THE AUTISTIC SURVIVAL GUIDE TO THERAPY

STEPH JONES

FOREWORDS BY
TONY ATTWOOD AND SARAH HENDRICKX

Jessica Kingsley Publishers
London and Philadelphia

First published in Great Britain in 2024 by Jessica Kingsley Publishers
An imprint of John Murray Press

Content Warning: This book talks about mental health with references
to suicide, suicidal ideation and suicidal thoughts.
Need support? Call 116 123 to speak to a Samaritan.

A CIP catalogue record for this title is available from the
British Library and the Library of Congress

ISBN 978 1 83997 731 2
eISBN 978 1 83997 730 5

Printed and bound in Great Britain by TJ Books Ltd

Jessica Kingsley Publishers
Carmelite House
50 Victoria Embankment
London EC4Y 0DZ

www.jkp.com

John Murray Press
Part of Hodder & Stoughton Ltd
An Hachette Company

The Autistic Survival Guide to Therapy

of related interest

Looking After Your Autistic Self
A Personalised Self-Care Approach to Managing Your Sensory and Emotional Well-Being
Niamh Garvey
ISBN 978 1 83997 560 8
eISBN 978 1 83997 561 5

Taking Off the Mask
Practical Exercises to Help Understand and Minimise the Effects of Autistic Camouflaging
Hannah Louise Belcher
ISBN 978 1 78775 589 5
eISBN 978 1 78775 590 1

So, I'm Autistic
An Introduction to Autism for Young Adults and Late Teens
Sarah O'Brien
ISBN 978 1 83997 226 3
eISBN 978 1 83997 227 0

This book is dedicated to my wonderful tribe of people who not only tolerate my weirdness but actively cherish and nurture it. Thank you for being ace. Beams.

My extra special love goes out to my lifelong best friend and partner in crime Collette Mary Theresa Montgomery Byrne (m'colleague, m'colleague), I really don't know where or who I would be without you. Troof nuggets. To my beautiful, funny, supportive and patient animal soulmate Ziggy, who I would be utterly lost without and whose fluffy snuggles make it all better again. And my sincerest gratitude to David Bowie, Kurt Cobain and all The Beatles for making me, me.

For my mum, who passed away too soon.

Contents

Foreword

BY TONY ATTWOOD

We need an autistic consumer's perspective of therapy. The experiences and themes described by Steph Jones will be invaluable for both therapists and autistic adults and their families. Her survival guide will also facilitate the development of new therapy models specifically designed for the autistic way of perceiving, thinking, learning and relating.

A therapist may have had limited training and previous and ongoing supervision in the adaptations to therapy to accommodate an autistic client's different way of perceiving, thinking, learning and relating.[1] As Steph Jones points out in this incredibly useful book, they may not be familiar with developing conceptualizations and theoretical models of autism, such as Theory of Mind, double empathy, camouflaging, autistic burnout, and being the authentic self. There may be the anticipation that conventional therapy will automatically be successful, but conventional therapy is based on the conventional, not the autistic mind.

Within therapy, alexithymia, which can be experienced by autistic people, can lead to difficulty answering the question, 'How do you

---

1   A longer version of this foreword is reproduced at the end of this book which details these.

feel about that?' or 'Why did you do that?' The autistic client is not evasive or obtuse but may have genuine difficulty answering the question due to alexithymia. However, creative therapies such as art, music and drama therapy, and journaling and typing rather than talking can be used to facilitate self-expression and self-exploration and incorporated into therapy to accommodate alexithymia.

Over time a therapist may be able to learn to 'read' their autistic client and vice versa, but there can be miscommunication and false assumptions. An autistic client may misinterpret the therapist's loud voice as an expression of anger rather than an adjustment of volume due to transitory background noise or the therapist may assume that a blank facial expression is a sign of a lack of comprehension.

The client's social history will probably include experiences of peer or work-colleague rejection, humiliation, bullying and teasing. This can lead to a generalized lack of trust, and it will take some time for an autistic client to trust the therapist and recognize their benevolent intentions.

Autism is associated with chronic high anxiety levels and one of the coping mechanisms for high anxiety is trying to control life experiences and maintain autonomy by avoiding demands experienced as overwhelming. An autistic client might perceive accepting therapy advice as surrendering autonomy to the therapist. Therapy can be adjusted to give the client choices to surrendering autonomy to the therapist, maintain a sense of autonomy and guide them to discover what they need to do rather than 'obey' the therapist.

The therapist must also determine if the autistic client's work and home life and suppressing and camouflaging autism are toxic to their mental health. Some environments are not 'autism friendly' with expectations that are difficult for the autistic person to achieve, a lack of understanding of autism in the family and workplace and expecting a level of socializing and endurance of aversive sensory experiences that contribute to autistic burnout. The therapist, therefore, has an ethical dilemma of using therapy and medication to encourage the tolerance of circumstances that will continue contributing to mental health issues, to put the client back in the 'lion's cage'. Therapy, as Steph Jones shows in this much needed book, can help determine the characteristics of an autism-friendly lifestyle and develop an autistic client's capacity to thrive rather than just survive. There may be the valuable creation of a new lifestyle with guidance and support from the therapist that increases resilience and authenticity.

Foreword

BY SARAH HENDRICKX

As an autistic person who has sought help, support and explanation from numerous therapists over my lifetime, this is the book that I wish I'd had several decades ago. Steph tells us that she wished the same and that's why she wrote it. What took her so long?

So much has changed in the understanding and diagnosis of autistic adults, and yet in order to find some respite and help, we have not had bespoke therapy to turn to and have had to resort to what is often a poor fit therapeutic model with a poor fit therapist who expects us to comprehend and adhere to their tried and tested methods. If we fail to do so, then surely that is our fault for not trying hard enough? Unsurprisingly, as Steph reports both from personal and professional experience, we end up feeling like we have not only 'failed' at life and thus sought therapy in the first place; but 'failed' at therapy too because we were unable to progress and be 'fixed'. This too is my own experience and that of working with others who have often sought numerous different approaches and individuals, only to find that nothing really worked and frequently made them feel worse – and poorer in the process.

Steph gives us plenty of science, stats and explanations, leading us through autism, its commonly misdiagnosed bedfellows, trauma and mental health ramifications via lived experience and academic research. I learned a lot and said 'A-ha' a lot (not related to memories of the shockingly handsome Norwegian pop trio). The list of red herrings and common misinterpretations by therapists for entirely rational autistic behaviours is a piece of genius. She then guides us through a range of therapeutic approaches and considers how and why (or not) these may suit (or not) an autistic client. And all written in a beautifully readable style.

Intertwined in all of this sensible, factual stuff, Steph takes us on a journey into her own therapy via her relationship with the highly recognizable 'Veronica', with characteristic Mancunian humour. Any autistic person who has dabbled in therapy knows Veronica.

All in all, this book is a glorious experience of fine writing, great information and actual joy. Who would have thought therapy could be so much fun?! Steph's book entirely endorses my years of experience of working with autistic adults who are desperate to find someone who can help make sense of this non-autistic world in which we live. I recommend it heartily to every single person who receives an autism diagnosis to save them the pain and the cost of choosing the wrong path towards a comfortable existence. Devour and cherish this book, people.

Acknowledgements

To help me on my quest I have assembled a crack team of autism experts from across the world – both neurodivergent and neurotypical – a collection of therapists, social workers, coaches, academics and support workers with a huge breadth of experience and knowledge to bring to the table. I would like to thank all the therapists and individuals who contributed to this project; your insights and honest discussions have been nothing short of eye-opening and I am immensely grateful for your collaboration:

Michelle Hunt, LMHC, NCC
Claire Ratcliffe, MBACP, UKCP Reg.
Mariano Hvozda, ADHD and Autism Coach
Louise Weston MA (Art Therapy) AThR, AdDipATh
    (Transpersonal Art Therapy), BA (Graphic Design)
Jonas Dunér, sociologist, legal healthcare curator and
    undergraduate psychotherapist
Jennifer Glacel, LCSW, RPT-S
Mairead Keogan, LMSW
Annette Eriksen, clinical counsellor, career coach and PhD
    candidate
Christin Fontes, Licensed Professional Counselor (LPC)
Annalise Hammerlund, MA, LPC
Jodie Hnatkovich, LPC
James Barrott (BA Hons, PG Dip, Dip Gestalt Psych, Cert Sup,
    PGCAP, MSc, MBACP, UKCP) (and my old Uni tutor!)

CL

Luis Reis

Shanna Kramer, MA, LPC

Olena Baeva

Carly Lacey

Katrina Healey

Eleanor Yarisse, LCSW, PMH-C

Dr. Megan Neff

Ali Cunningham Abbott, PhD, LMHC, QS

Darren Wall

Debbie Palmer, an autistic specialist speech and language therapist, diagnostic clinician and neurodevelopmental specialist

Stephen (my last therapist!)

Also, for help in preparing this book, my great big mahoosive thanks to Professor Tony Attwood, Sarah Hendrickx, Paul Micallef, Samantha Stein, Dr. Naomi Fisher, Amelia Hill, Jannine Duffy (my B of the bang!), Penny Lawson, Debbie Palmer, my clients (both past and present), my social media followers, and to you – the neurodivergent community.

Disclaimer

Whilst this book aims to provide you with a range of useful information and support around the themes of therapy, autism and mental health, it should not be taken as a substitute for therapy or regarded as a recommendation to take any particular course of action. This book is for educational purposes only and is not medical or mental health advice, nor does it constitute any treatment plan. The opinions offered in this book (mine and those who contributed) are just that, opinions. Remember, **you** are the expert in your own life. There is no one-size-fits-all approach to therapy and no two people are alike. It would be impossible to write a book which appeals to every single autistic person, but I have done my best to ensure it remains as inclusive as possible.

Preface

I suppose it makes sense to explain why I decided to write this book and what sparked it all off. After learning I was autistic at the grand old age of 41, I decided to set up an Instagram account to make some friends and figure out what the hell being autistic actually meant. Despite being the kind of person who generally shuns social media, I found myself immersed in a brand new world, full of others who seemed to be describing my perception of the world.

I went from feeling like I was the only mad woman in the village to realizing actually, I'd just been in the wrong village. My account grew extremely quickly, and rather than just using it as a space to connect with others I started to provide psychoeducation around autism, mental health and therapy – essentially translating some of the hard-to-digest research into snappy little soundbites with my anecdotal overshares.

One of the things I find particularly frustrating (although that does seem to be changing slowly) is that the narrative about autism is often not in **our** hands. Whilst it may be very useful for me to learn about autism from textbooks, experts and researchers, I know in my heart that experientially I will learn more from my peers. That isn't to take away from the passion and energy that non-autistic professionals have to contribute, but put simply, you want to know the best places to go on holiday – ask a local.

After an initial shout-out on my page asking for autistic people to describe their experiences in therapy (did it help or did it harm?), I was inundated with a bucket load of emails, messages and comments. Your brave, raw and relatable stories provide the heart to this work, and it is my hope that others may relate to your experiences and feel less alone. I know from my own journey that, whilst I cannot undo the pain and trauma caused by damaging therapy, I can find comfort, wisdom and validation in connecting with others who have been through similar. I can feel seen and answer that niggling voice at the back of my mind, 'Was it them, or was it me?'

The neurotypical textbooks tend to focus on autism through the eyes of a medical disorder with its symptoms, dysfunctions and deficits. They often have such a narrow bandwidth of what it is to be autistic that it's a bit like suggesting there is only one type of dog in existence. If all you know about dogs is that they come in the shape of a golden retriever, you're probably not very likely to let Mr. Pug into the Kennel Club. The media tends to shape what we know, and without broader representation of the whole spectrum to educate us, there will be many a pug that gets into its arthritic wobbly days wondering why it's a pretty rubbish cat. Establishment, take note and start to listen to the community. You might just learn a thing or two.

Out of gratitude and deep respect I have incorporated as many of your voices as possible, although all personal details have been changed to protect privacy. Without your contributions there would be **no book**. You asked me to write this, and believe me when I say I sincerely hope I do you justice in bringing your issues and concerns to a wider audience.

With deepest thanks.

Steph (www.instagram.com/Autistic_Therapist)

INTRODUCTION

WHY THIS BOOK?

This is the book I wish I'd read 20 years ago, before I started my therapy journey.

This is the book that would've saved me nine different therapists, decades of self-analysis, thousands of pounds, twelve different doctors and untold amounts of pain, frustration and trauma. It's not so much that I regret my journey – without it I wouldn't know anything about psychology, I wouldn't be a therapist and I certainly wouldn't be the person I am today – but in spending a lifetime looking for the right answers in the wrong places I've become an accidental expert.

The sad thing is, in that all those years of being a therapee (is that even a word? If not let's use it anyway) sat in a variety of chairs across from nodding strangers scribbling my secrets into notepads, not **one single therapist** suggested I might be autistic. It's been put forward that maybe all my problems originated from childhood trauma, stress, depression, anxiety, maybe bipolar, maybe some kind of personality disorder. Maybe there's nothing wrong with me at all and that I'm just an attention-seeking hypochondriac? Or maybe I just think too much, am too sensitive and need to grow a thicker skin? In hindsight (which is always irritatingly perfect) I have spent much of my life squashing my square peg into a round hole and wondering why nothing really worked. Turns out you can't cure a neurotype.

WHO IS THIS BOOK FOR?

It's an alarming but true fact that many late-diagnosed adults don't discover they are autistic until the proverbial shit hits the fan. It's almost like we navigated the first few chapters of life reasonably well (naturally battle-scarred) but generally intact. Then one day, for whatever reason, life becomes completely untenable and a nuclear-scale burnout occurs. Everything that you could do before seems practically impossible now – skills are lost, even the will is lost. We grind to a standstill as we realize there is **no more coal** to fuel the engine.

As we scratch our heads and wonder why our functioning has shrunk like Alice Through the Looking-Glass nibbling on a plate of dubious cakes labelled 'Watch it, love, things might get real small', we can't help but ask ourselves why we've used up so much coal in the first place doing normal everyday stuff. On the weighing scales of life, our demands now vastly exceed our capacity and we collapse into little broken heaps of people. Sometimes crying, sometimes screaming, sometimes just blankly staring into space – every which way, there is nothing left to give.

At this point most of us will do the sensible thing and drag ourselves to the nearest doctor who will peer over their spectacles and inform us that we're showing symptoms of stress, anxiety and clinical depression. We nod in compliant agreement and take the advice to rest, exercise and eat well, and dutifully cash in our prescriptions.

We may circle this loop for years wondering why things aren't improving for us. We try **everything**. We've eliminated so many food groups that we may as well live on bread (gluten-free, naturally) and water. We rattle with costly supplements. We pray to the gods of self-help, we redesign our days to include nap times and feel privately irritated that our 82-year old neighbour has more energy than we do.

It may take several trips around the sun, round and around the revolving door of mental health services, until one day we stumble across some game-changing information. We realize that we might be **autistic**. From this new perspective we begin to ask ourselves questions: Do I even have mental health issues, or am I simply exhibiting a completely relative reaction to living in a world which wasn't designed for me? Have I been misdiagnosed? Cause or symptom? Trauma or autism? Our heads spin with possibilities which seem impossible to answer.

Of course, this book isn't only for the late-diagnosed amongst us, it is for those who have known for as long as they can remember, the self-diagnosed, and those who may have an inkling but not yet fallen deep into the rabbit hole of research. Ultimately this is a book for those who seek to understand themselves.

Autistic spectrum disorder (ASD) has been neatly diagnostically categorized into three different areas to reflect the amount of support required:

- ASD1 = needs support
- ASD2 = requires substantial support
- ASD3 = requires very substantial support

But it simply isn't possible to cover all issues relating to all presentations and permutations of a neurological difference. Personally I'm not so keen on functioning labels, which can often feel a bit misleading (although I respect anyone's decision to self-identify in whatever way they choose). To my mind **high-functioning autism** could imply that we're hardly autistic at all (like a mild case of Ebola), thereby minimizing many of the invisible struggles we face. Likewise for **low-functioning autism**, where someone's strengths and abilities could be overlooked.

A high ability to mask and pass for 'normal' typically gives everyone the impression that your well-crafted neurotypical-esque personality is who you are 24/7, and it's doubtful that others will understand that your internal experience may be more like sitting in the trenches in 1916, psyching yourself to go over the top with little more than a fidget spinner. However, for the sake of this book, I will make the assumption that you are willing, eligible and prepared to engage in traditional psychological therapies and that you wish to learn more about their potential benefits and limitations.

Looking after our own

Sometimes when I'm mooching about online I feel a bit frustrated about the way autism is discussed by certain voices. It's as if there are particular rules one is expected to abide by (if one is to autisté correctly) which to me, feels far too dogmatic. Each week I receive dozens of distressing messages from often vulnerable, impressionable and confused neurodivergent people asking me what the correct protocol is (like they didn't receive their membership welcome pack in the post) absolutely terrified of being cancelled.

As a minority group we know all too well what it is to feel oppressed by society, yet sadly I witness the same traumatic them-and-us dynamic play out within our own community. If you've gone your whole life feeling that you've had to conform, deny your authenticity and supress your true voice, it seems very disconcerting to me that people are feeling scared about treading on eggshells in a space which should be there to lift you up.

I worry that there may be parts of this book that you can't connect with. Maybe you'll find my words clumsy, maybe I'll miss out an important point, maybe I'll make (gasp, shock horror!) a mistake! But we have to learn to be okay with people getting things wrong and not wiping them off the face of the earth for having a different opinion. Because the alternative is, well, fascism. Identifying culturally with a group doesn't mean you need to trade your individuality.

I would hate for anyone to assume that I exist in some Tony Robbins-esque peak state simply because I'm a therapist. At the end of the day, I'm still autistic. My meltdowns and shutdowns didn't suddenly evaporate on graduation day, nor am I some Insta-perfect bearded guru who grew up in wealthy privilege (rather, the only child of a single parent narcissistic alcoholic raised in a deprived area of northern England). In fact, as I write this, I am several months into a pernicious autistic burnout, which is the culmination of unavoidable personal issues, a mounting workload and Covid-19. None of us are immune to life and to the best of my knowledge nobody has hacked autism.

Sometimes what we say as autistic people gets a bit lost in translation when speaking to neurotypical folk. It's not that they don't necessarily hear us, but our well-chosen descriptive words seem nevertheless to be misinterpreted. I've had to learn the hard way that not all therapists are made equal and that expensive training, having letters after your name and a fancy office doesn't necessarily make you good at your job.

We matter

Whilst I don't anticipate that this book will solve all your problems (now wouldn't **that** be a good read?!), I still hope it will provide valuable insights into the mental health of a neurodivergent operating system, and give you the knowledge to discern therapy help from therapy harm. Let's be honest, reading about this kind of stuff can sometimes feel, well, a bit depressing, but it is my sincere wish that you will get to the end feeling not only clearer, better informed and well-prepared to go into therapeutic battle (should any battle occur) but possibly even take to the streets banging pots and pans, waving flags made out of Granny's bloomers and shouting '**The revolution is coming!**' Because it should.

Neurodivergent people shouldn't be an add-on or adaptive after-thought to traditional therapies not designed for our brains in the first place. We shouldn't **have** to buy a book to help us navigate the already bloody confusing world of psychological support services, and we should most definitely, categorically, unquestionably **not** feel lost in translation when we are doing our level best to be seen, heard and understood.

We all know that being in therapy isn't easy. Healing (despite how spa-like the word sounds) can be an uprooting, non-linear and frustrating process, more like giving birth to a baby grand piano. It is after all the space where we painfully deconstruct all the difficult pieces of our lives causing problems for us in the here and now. But we should remain vigilant to **what** is upsetting us in therapy – processing the challenging subject material or the therapeutic relationship itself?

We ask our clients to 'trust in the process' and I totally believe that, but it doesn't mean we should put blind faith in a relationship that doesn't feel right. Therapy isn't like going to the gym (no pain, no gain!), and dedicated perseverance doesn't always guarantee the Holy Grail if you're following the wrong map.

We enter into psychological care with a desire to feel better. We are vulnerable and said to be in a 'state of incongruence'. There is something we don't quite understand but we are bright and eager to figure it out. As noble a quest as this may seem, it also puts us in the path of potential harm, because if you don't know how to read the red flags in therapy, how can you tell when things aren't going so well?

This isn't an anti-therapy book ('cause well, duh, I **am** a therapist), nor should it be taken as a series of 'alternative facts' to counter something your therapist says that is actually true but you just didn't want to hear. Put simply, **this isn't about cancelling your therapist because they disagree with you**, but it is about providing a sense of balance, self-awareness and perspective so that we don't leave therapy with only half a story about who we are.

If being honest and sharing my experiences can help someone else, I'm all in, and to be honest I think I would have probably done a lot better in therapy over the years had my therapists said, 'You know what, Steph, I feel like that too,' instead of making me feel so alone and damaged. I praise all those courageous mental health workers who dare to normalize emotions, whose use of spontaneous and relevant self-disclosure gives patients Eureka![1] moments, helping them to discover new solutions to old problems. Thank you for not hiding in your ivory towers and for getting messy in the mud with us.

It is my hope that in sharing my own personal story of dodgy therapy, you may begin to recognize some of the danger signs. For the therapists reading this book, I urge you to take these accounts and case studies as a masterclass in how **not** to do autistic therapy, to set aside any preconceived ideas you may have; to be humble, open and learn to see to your client with a fresh pair of eyes.

---

1   Totally irrelevant but interesting anyway: the word 'Eureka' comes from the Greek word 'heurēka', which means 'I have found it' and is thought to have been bellowed by Archimedes when he discovered a way of determining gold purity.

**For the professionals reading this,
or the ones you're working with**

To support any professionals who might be reading this book, or who the reader might be working with, at the back of this book I have included a context guide to my story which deconstructs the sessions and shows you exactly where I am clearly describing my undiagnosed autism to my therapist. Naturally we come in all flavours, so this only represents my particular version of toffee and vanilla, but it's a start at the very least, and something to get conversations going in your training workshops.

As an undiagnosed autistic person at the time, I was completely powerless and defenceless at the mercy of clinicians arrogant enough to assume they knew me better than I knew myself. I'm definitely not the first autistic person to be traumatized in the pursuit of healing (as this book clearly demonstrates) and certainly won't be the last.

ROADMAP TO THE SURVIVAL GUIDE

I suspect this is the bit where I should do a little tour guide piece at the front of the bus, and let you know where we'll be visiting as we wind through the pages. A packet of gummy bears is now being passed through the aisles, please adjust your headrest to a comfortable position, sit back and relax.

Chapter 1 will have a look at some of the reasons we are misdiagnosed and misunderstood, laying out the foundations for the book. Because unless we know we are autistic, how are we to receive the right level of care? We will explore why clinicians are failing to recognize the somewhat obvious signs in us and their medical tendencies to incorrectly diagnose us with all manner of psychological disturbances we don't have.

There's a bigger call to action here in that the powers that be really need to get their act together and start learning about autism from the autistic community. A one-hour training course at doctor school does not equate to a lifetime of living with a condition. This really isn't anybody's fault, I received zero training on my psychotherapy course too, but we have to draw the line somewhere, weaponized incompetence is unacceptable.

Chapter 2 builds on this and takes a look at how trauma interacts with an autistic brain. It poses the questions: What **is** trauma? Are we at a greater risk from a biological and neurological perspective (science-y facts for the geeks out there)? Also what **is** complex post-traumatic stress disorder (CPTSD) and how similar is it to autism? (Spoiler alert: frighteningly similar on paper as it turns out.)

It concerns me greatly that many professionals still seem to think that autism is a mental health issue, rather than a brain structural and processing difference (think iPhone and Android). And it concerns me that to be taken seriously by our doctors we must often go to ridiculous lengths to assert our case – essentially delivering a free clinical workshop entitled 'The Antiquated Perspectives of Autism'.

Chapter 3 is a technical mapping of our perceptual human experiences if you like, so that the average person may start to understand that we are not a neurotypical brain with a bit of autism in it (like a bit of bread stuck in your teeth) but a totally different neurotype with unique gadgets and gizmos. Unfortunately, as this chapter will show, one of the biggest issues we are likely to encounter (in life, not just the therapy room) is around being understood. And what happens when human beings are continually misunderstood, invalidated and gaslighted into thinking their thoughts and feelings are wrong? That's right, folks, you guessed it – **trauma**! Houston, we have a link.

The big problem is that not only are many of us dealing with an invisible condition, but we are doing so in a culture which doesn't think like us or value the same things. The neuronormative society that we exist in fills us with ideas about who we **should** be from day one, telling us what success looks like, what we are supposed to enjoy doing with our leisure time, how to look, how to behave, how to communicate if we are to be liked by others – the list goes on. All of which may feel completely out of alignment with who we really are, forcing us into unconscious masks of supressed pain. And what happens when a human being supresses who they really are? That's right folks, even more **trauma**!

Therapy also encourages us to get in touch with our feelings if we are to start feeling better – but what if we are unable to access them fully due to sensory differences such as alexithymia or synaesthesia? How can we be expected to label emotions if we experience them in abstract, or have to translate words to pictures? How can our therapist even know what we are talking about? Will we become even more traumatized in therapy due to this kind of communication breakdown?

Chapter 4 is a bit longer than the others and you might decide to skip this part or just find the bits that relate to your own situation. The chapter will look at the typical kinds of issues you might be having problems with, for example social anxiety, fatigue, anxiety, depression, identity. It will explore how the **presenting surface psychological symptoms** may actually be more indicative of hidden autism and, as you might expect, may have a completely different pathway to reducing distress and improving our quality of life. Put simply, are your mental health issues secondary to undiagnosed and/or supressed autism? On paper, autistic burnout and depression might look identical, but encouraging a burnt-out neurodivergent person to 'get out more and do more stuff' is very likely to do more harm than good.

Chapter 5 sets out the nuts and bolts of how to spot an unsuitable therapist using a few humorous examples of types you probably want to avoid (trust me, I've met them all). Many of us struggle with correctly interpreting social situations, which can make it all the more difficult to recognize the danger signs. Although I think it's fair to say that the majority of practitioners in the caring professions are drawn to their vocation out of a genuine desire to help others, it's important that we stay vigilant – not everyone has good intentions and many of us have learned this the hard way.

I look back to my early life and reflect on just how naïve I really was (even though I thought I knew it all at the time) compared to how suspicious and cynical I am now of just about everyone. I'm not saying that's a positive position to be in either, but it means my boundaries are much clearer, I can pre-empt danger, and that if my gut says no, it's a **no**.

Chapter 6 expands on how we may be unintentionally harmed in therapy. It will look at several therapeutic concepts which just do not apply to us, but which some therapists use willy-nilly anyway. The chapter explores themes such as reframing, graded exposure, the window of tolerance, therapeutic ruptures, attachment theory, session dialogue and body-language, arguing that clinical assumptions based on traditional therapies (created for neurotypical people) may put us in the path of serious harm as we are taught to override our internal experiences to appear more 'normal'.

If the chapters to date fill you with worry and dread, fear ye not, Chapter 7 to the rescue! This section pools together a vast amount of clinical experience and suggestions from **actually autistic therapists** and coaches across the world, exploring some of the better and safer options. Fortunately there's loads of approaches to look into, and I hope this part of the book allows you to think about what would be best for **you**.

Whenever someone asks me for a therapist recommendation I always explain to them that choosing a practitioner is a bit like going on a date – it's an entirely subjective experience and largely comes down to the relationship. What if I were to make a suggestion of a 'good' therapist and the client didn't gel with them? How might they feel about themselves under those circumstances? Chapter 7 provides an easy-to-understand layman's critique (begone confusing words!) on many of the well-known evidence-based approaches (e.g. cognitive and behavioural, psychoanalysis and psychodynamic, humanistic) as well as looking into other areas such as coaching, mentoring, creative therapies, music, arts, nature and even psychedelics.

The chapter also asks whether we might be better off having a neurodivergent therapist. What are the benefits and pitfalls of this? Will we feel better understood, or will the practitioner share the same blind spots? Pulling it all together this chapter concludes with a Top 10 list (insert 'Top of the Pops' music here) compiled by the autistic therapists on how to choose a decent therapist. Bosh!

The final chapter of the book, which I wrote before my fingers resigned and my eyes went on holiday, will look at a number of additional and important themes. These include types of neurodivergent accommodations you might like to ask for in sessions, and other non-therapy options for your healing journey, because let's face it therapy isn't accessible to everyone but good mental health is non-negotiable really. All the responses from my Instagram self-care shout-out live here.

Oh and one last thing, this is probably the part where I should say (clears throat, picks up megaphone...) the storyline that runs throughout this book is a work of fiction. Veronica isn't a real person – thankfully you won't bump into her in your search for a therapist or in your local Tesco. But she **is** a composite of many therapists, of different genders, that I have heard of and sadly, met. Any similarities to persons living or dead or actual events is purely coincidental, much in the same way Michael Jackson's werewolf in 'Thriller' isn't actually real.

Public service announcement over, enjoy the book!

Chapter 1

MYTHS, MISDIAGNOSED AND MISUNDERSTOOD

This has to be my last dalliance with therapy.

You can't say I haven't tried, I've been in and out of beige-coloured counselling offices for the last 20 years. When things haven't been working out I've tried addressing it with therapists, changing therapists, changing the type of therapy, but nothing ever seems to help me feel better. I am starting to resent parting with my hard-earned dosh at the end of a session.

There are only so many times you can go over early childhood traumatic memories, and it feels like there's not a stone left unturned in my Google-mapped psyche. It's not to say my ex-therapists have in themselves been bad, but it's often felt like we've been talking at cross-purposes. What I say and how **they** interpret me seems to be at odds, and I get the sense they have me labelled as a 'difficult patient'. Through therapy, the image I have of myself is that of a person who is too sensitive, too reactive, too resistant, too independent, too much of a thinker. Overall, I see myself as too much.

Working from this miserable starting point, I cobble together a sketchy narrative of my life which meanders through a hearty collection of woes in which my mother is to blame for just about everything, including a drop in the FTSE 100 Index.

The worst bit is giving up on one therapist and starting afresh with another knowing full well they are going to draw the exact same conclusions, taking you right back to where you started. There are no new connections to be made in this eternal game of Freudian Snakes and Ladders, but I convince myself that if I just keep going and throw more time and money at it, then one day I will uncover the psychological equivalent of life on Mars and live happily ever after. Only right now I don't feel very (therapy buzzword alert) 'resilient', despite facing the fear and doing it anyway. Every. Single. Day. It's exhausting to adult.

I enjoy driving to therapy. It's a nice, leafy jaunt, and you pass lots of big posh houses on the way that I could never possibly afford. People around here are well-groomed and look like they're on the way to important job interviews even when they're just putting the bins out. But as soon as I arrive at my therapist's office my heart sinks. For starters you have to buzz an intercom to be let in ('Hiiiiya, it's Steph, I'm here to see Veronica...?'). But you never get an answer back leaving you feeling a bit silly every time. I imagine a snooty suited French concierge sat in a dingy basement lit by a single swinging ten-watt bulb deciding the fate of all who dare to buzz. Not today, Stephanie. You've been a bad girl.

The building is occupied by various other businesses, and I feel irritated that I have to pass the prying eyes of the staff who work there. Accountants and solicitors, that sort of thing – people who stop talking when you walk past the photocopier and make silent judgements on your Monday morning attire. As I shuffle down the long corridor of shame I eventually arrive at Veronica's door and sit on a small burgundy plastic chair.

It is 10:59am. Veronica has never let me in before 11 o'clock on the dot, and I reflect on how this sends a powerful message in therapy – we are teaching clients that boundaries matter. Such rules are there to impose a proper structure and purpose and make sure that everyone knows where they stand. I am quite happy with the formality of this arrangement, even if I do feel a bit like a dog waiting to eat a biscuit off its nose.

At 11 o'clock and 14 seconds Veronica opens the door in complete silence, holds it wide open and nods me inside, her gesture being slightly reminiscent of a 17th-century Transylvanian butler. Before I sit down on the massive throne-like chair with its ridiculously tall and uncomfortable back, I open the proceedings with my usual cheerful, 'Y'alright?' Such is the correct protocol if you grew up in the north of England.

'Why do you always insist on asking me that question when you know I won't answer?' she clipped in a sharp tone.

'Err... that's just what you say – how you greet! I'm Man-cun-ian!' I chirrup, desperately attempting to keep things breezy. Quietly ignoring the fact I feel like I've just been kicked in the stomach by a hormonal donkey.

Veronica begins to pick fluff off her sleeve and raises her eyebrows. 'I work with patients from Manchester all the time and they don't say that. I've never met anyone who says that.'

I am stunned by Veronica's snappy response to my polite attempt at a hello and feel crestfallen. I was only trying to be friendly but instead I'm being covertly accused of a boundary violation. I know how this stuff works. I've got my therapist badges.

Her prickly tone has completely sent me under (she doesn't seem to know what that means either) and I feel myself drowning in 'the bad place'. I force myself to engage in conversation, trying with Jedi-like mind power to remember the well-prepared reasons I'm here in the first place, but I just can't get back on firm footing now – her vibe has knocked me off my axis.

Annoyingly I find myself zoning out, vacantly gazing into the distance fixated on a tiny brown sparrow in a tree. I expect she thinks this performance is me sulking, being passive-aggressive, childishly refusing to communicate like an adult, but the truth is I cannot wade through the trance-like treacle which has accumulated in my brain and fake normalcy.

I have been told that what is happening is something called 'dissociation' – an automatic nervous system trauma-based response – yet to me it can happen anytime. When it happens it's more like I've gone on a kind of power save mode yet still being completely present in my mind and body. Sometimes it feels quite nice and I can lose myself staring at a blank wall for a full hour in a kind of guru-level meditative state. I've noticed my little cousin do it too, but he hasn't even gone through any trauma. He's only five.

I try to push though this invisible wall of mutism, even summoning up amusing images of Liam Gallagher doing a wobbly side dance, front teeth over bottom lip (which I know you just tried) and sticking the middle finger up at her. I do not feel understood, I do not feel believed – she is healthy and right, and I am dysfunctional and wrong.

In **her** mind we are embroiled in some kind of power struggle in which I am trying to defeat my mother. It's a bit like being served a plate of horse dung in a fancy restaurant, but when you complain to the waiter they tell you your palette isn't refined enough. Dead parrot sketch, much?

Attempting to regain composure I take a deep breath, internally count to ten and adjust my throne so that it is perfectly straight and parallel to her chair. I do this every week and at this stage I am not clear whether the cleaner arranges it at such an exasperating and blatantly incorrect angle or if Veronica is testing me. If my chair is not in the correct position all I can think about for the session is that the furniture is **wrong**. Any more than this I cannot say, although a preliminary exploration of the issue took us to reflect on my obsessive, controlling and neurotic tendencies.

WHAT'S IN A NAME?

Whilst carrying out the initial research for this book I began to notice the kind of language that is often used to describe autism:

- abnormal
- atypical
- impaired
- deficits
- disorder
- lack of abilities
- difficulties
- poorly integrated
- socially unaware
- disturbances.

It's hardly surprising that the general public has such a narrow view of what it is to be autistic if all they are exposed to are negative explanations, one-dimensional journalism (autism 'strikes' 1 in

44 kids, apparently) and comedic television characters which only serve to perpetuate stereotypes.

When I first discovered I was neurodivergent, many well-meaning individuals shocked me with their initial responses: But you don't look autistic! Are you sure? You seem so normal! Shall I call you Rainman now?! After sharing the news with a neighbour I'd known for almost a decade I noticed how she suddenly began to speak much softer and slower in the same way some patronizing buffoons choose to speak to elderly people (my Nana once remarked, 'Why do people do that, Steph? I'm deaf not stupid.'). My neighbour's reaction, like many of the others I received, revealed a much darker lesser spoken perception of autism – that there's clearly something wrong with my upstairs department.

WHAT THE HELL IS AUTISM ANYWAY?

Let's just pause for a moment and think about what autism actually is in order to try and give ourselves some broader context. Autism is not a disease, nor is it a mental health issue we need to cure (although we may also struggle with our mental health but more on that later). The word autism derives from the Greek words 'autós' meaning self (aut) and '–ismós' (ism) meaning state, and was first coined in 1911 by a Swiss psychiatrist called Paul Eugen Bleuler (who dropped the name Paul) as a way to describe a symptom of severe schizophrenia.

According to Paul-not-Paul, autistic thinking was a desire to avoid reality, essentially living in a dream world of internal fantasies and hallucinations (Bleuler 1950). However, over subsequent decades the word began to lose its original meaning and by 1972 Sir Michael Rutter (also known as the father of child psychology, bit like James Brown being the Godfather of Soul) had decided that autism meant that the, 'autistic child has a deficiency of fantasy rather than an excess'.

Fast forward a bit and the neurobiologists will have you believe that autism is actually a, 'polygenetic developmental neurobiologic disorder with multiorgan system involvement' involving 'central nervous system dysfunction' (Minshew and Williams 2007). Hmm. Not many people asking actually autistic people so far, is there? It reminds me of a quote in the film 'Good Will Hunting', where Will's therapist, Sean (played by the genius that was Robin Williams) tells Will that whilst he might intellectually **know** everything there is to know about Michelangelo including his inside leg measurements (I made that up, that isn't said), he still wouldn't have a clue about what it **smells** like in the Sistine Chapel.

Autism is a neurological difference, meaning that we process information differently. Not better, not worse, just differently. It is not measurable on a straight line continuum from 'a little bit autistic' to 'very autistic' and is far more like plotting unique data on a radar chart. Person A might have a relatively low score when it comes to challenges with verbal communication but score highly on sensory issues. Person B might have a low score when it comes to engaging in repetitive behaviours (i.e. doesn't stim very much) but struggle a great deal with understanding the intentions of others. It is practically impossible to pigeonhole 1% (maybe more) of the world's population into neat little boxes, particularly when we introduce other elements to the mix such as environmental factors, genetics, trauma, health, interpersonal dynamics, personality, privilege, and introverted/extroverted preferences.

WHAT AUTISM SURE AS HELL IS NOT

Before I understood anything about neurodiversity I naturally assumed that all my issues were psychological and something to be fixed in therapy. From an early age I recognized that I was different to others but couldn't put my finger on the reason why. I have fond memories of primary school where I was always top of the class and could get away with bossing around other children to play **my** games, **my** way. But as soon as puberty hit everything seemed to change.

I found myself socially confused and could not fathom out for the life of me why all of a sudden my 12-year-old classmates (seemingly overnight) were dead against making up hilarious rude poems and improvising scenes from 'Neighbours' during lunch breaks. And why they were more interested in being 'cool', grown up and part of the mob. I felt like I was living in 'Invasion of the Bodysnatchers'.

'God Steph, you're so immature,' they would taunt as I refused to join in with the latest fad or trend. This week we're all into Take That! They're hot. Oh actually, no, that's soooo last week now. This week, we're all into East 17 and we all hate Gary Barlow... From my perspective it seemed like everyone had lost the ability to think for themselves and were sailing on a kind of invisible sheep-culture tide I wasn't part of.

College days were even worse as I couldn't figure out which group I belonged to and found myself walking around corridors at break times looking 'very busy' (but secretly just avoiding interactions). Imagine a world where you didn't have a smartphone to keep you occupied?

In my early twenties, drugs and alcohol became a godsend and helped my social challenges to practically evaporate. In fact, being 'a bit weird' in the late 1990s where alternative culture was mainstream actually gave me extra points in the popularity contest of life. But as those halcyon days and social mores shifted to give way to more mundane things like going to work, having a place to live, and adulting well enough to ensure you stayed alive, I quickly realized I was out of my depth.

My doctor at the time decided I had social anxiety and put me on antidepressants, which contrary to what the name suggests actually made me very very depressed. Memories of lying in the middle of the road on a busy Saturday afternoon, hysterical, clutching a bottle of vodka and listening to The Smiths still haunt me to this day.

(By the way, anybody featured in a quotation bubble box throughout the rest of this book isn't me, it's our brilliant contributors.)

'Before I was correctly diagnosed I had been treated for an impressive array of conditions and slowly felt my life was sliding away from me. I was told I had anxiety, depression, obsessive compulsive disorder, social anxiety, post-traumatic stress disorder, and later on borderline personality disorder (BPD). The treatment for that felt like the worst because it required me to attend regular group sessions which I found really overwhelming from a sensory position and also really frightening because there were a lot of dysregulated people in the group starting arguments. I had no idea what I was doing there.'

My first ever post on Instagram was a curious shout-out asking what conditions autistic people had been diagnosed with before they were correctly identified. Together we racked up an impressive laundry list including:

- Complex post-traumatic stress disorder (CPTSD)
- Post-traumatic stress disorder (PTSD)
- Emotionally unstable personality disorder (EUPD) also known as borderline personality disorder (BPD)
- Eating disorders
- Schizoaffective disorder
- Agoraphobia
- Panic disorder
- Sensitivity disturbances
- Bipolar disorder
- Schizophrenia
- Histrionic personality disorder
- Antisocial personality disorder
- Dysthymia (due to flat affect)
- Attachment disorders
- Adjustment disorders
- Neurosis
- Hypochondria
- Psychosomatic illnesses
- Attention deficit/hyperactivity disorder (ADD/ADHD)
- Depression
- Anxiety
- Stress
- Obsessive compulsive disorder
- Antisocial or narcissistic personality disorders
- Myalgic encephalomyelitis/chronic fatigue syndrome (ME/CFS)
- Munchausen's syndrome.

One respondent mentioned they were told it was 'part of being a woman', another remarked it was thought to be 'all in my head'. Christin Fontes, a Licensed Professional Counselor, also shared how:

After receiving my diagnosis I have had a-ha moments **daily** about things that I thought were fixed parts of my personality that are actually signs and symptoms of autism. How much of this hurt could have been avoided? How much of it shapes the way I show up in the world today? What will it take for me to return to the girl that arrived here originally on the day of my birth? Do I have what it takes to heal, or is the damage done? The most exciting part of this trauma is that a lot of it happened at the hands of people who 'meant the best'. It wasn't malicious, but it was still harmful. How does one reckon that? I was a child.

TRAINING MATTERS

As I pored over my personal collection of counselling and psychotherapy books to help me pull this all together, something became glaringly obvious; **not one single text mentioned autism.**

This begs the critical question: How can psychological interventions claim to help neurodivergent people if our basic operating systems have not been taken into consideration in terms of the theory? Is the neurodivergent mind simply an add-on to traditional therapy design and therefore flawed from the outset? One anonymous autistic therapist I spoke with confided in me just how little they learned about autism on their training course.

At one point in my first year internship, I had a client who was likely autistic and undiagnosed, and used his case to write a paper describing a case study. I had diagnosed him with social anxiety and depression, and when I turned in my paper my professor pointed out that he might be autistic, but said he didn't have much background in autism and couldn't be that helpful. I went to the supervisor of that internship and mentioned the same thing, and she also did not know what to do. I was unable to find someone who could help figure out how he might get assessed or what services might be helpful, which was quite heart breaking since this client was a teen who had dropped out of school due to social issues, and was going to a poorly run and underfunded General Educational Development programme that provided no assistance to students with disabilities. Afterwards, I put a lot more effort into learning about autism since it was not coming up in my classes, and found a summer job working with autistic teens. Most of my information comes from books and social media accounts.

This pervasive pattern of poor, limited or non-existent training cropped up on nearly all of the research questionnaires completed by our cohort of neurodivergent professionals, with UK-based therapist and supervisor Kat Healey feeling that it was disappointing not to learn more in class, estimating that around 40% of her clients are probably autistic. Another professional commented:

It was not included in any of my education other than teaching about ABA (Applied Behaviour Analysis) as the treatment and moving on quickly. Both autism and ADHD were presented as 'unhelpable' and clients that are hard to 'fix'. – therapist Michelle Hunt

I'm glad to say that we live in very different times to the world I grew up in (the gradual destigmatization of mental health for a start) yet it does appear that there are some glaringly inherent problems in the system when it comes to gaps in practitioner knowledge.

> I remember hearing one story from a client saying the therapist believed they couldn't be autistic because they made eye-contact. Another client said their previous therapist said, 'everyone's a little autistic'. There's a loss of hope and trust in the mental health care system because there's very little training from educational institutions/employers, and therapists don't always take the effort to fill that gap and learn. – therapist Mairead Keogan

I have heard many stories of suspected autistic patients literally having to convince their GP to refer them for an assessment, often taking along chapters of printed evidence to substantiate their opinion. Whilst the medical and psychological establishments continue to operate from an outdated perspective of what autism is (e.g. it only affects boys, you can't make eye-contact, you can't do empathy, you must like memorizing train timetables, collecting stamps and lining things up) huge numbers of us stand little chance of being heard.

Whilst there is much written about how people assigned female at birth tend to go undiagnosed, I personally don't see this exclusively as a gender issue. I work with plenty of individuals on a daily basis (including males and non-binary folk) who simply by not fitting the autism typecast have also been missed, mislabelled and mistreated.

Unfortunately the patient/professional relationship dynamic is innately imbalanced to start with, and not every physician is open to their antiquated views, unexplored ableism and misinterpretations being corrected. One of my good colleagues (who wishes to remain anonymous because they are not openly autistic in their work) shared:

> I remember overhearing a colleague talking about a patient once, it was all, 'Aw, the poor thing, it must be awful for them having autism.' It felt very 'other' even though there was no real ill-intention behind it, but it made me realize it wasn't safe to put myself out there professionally as an autistic person if we're regarded as lesser in some people's eyes. I'm good at my job because I'm autistic and it gives me a particular skill set others don't have (like pattern recognition, a photographic memory, noticing small details which most miss) and I'd hate for colleagues to think I do well in spite of my diagnosis.

Professor Tony Attwood is a well-loved British psychologist with an illustrious career spanning over five decades and generally considered to be one of the world's foremost experts on autism spectrum disorder. Early last summer I had the pleasure of chatting with Tony (UK to Australia!) who had so many interesting things to say I could probably write a second book on it! His quotes will feature throughout the chapters but with regard to training he feels that the UK is probably much further ahead than Australia or the US, summarizing it perfectly:

> Clinicians by definition see when autism is going wrong, they don't see it when it's going right, because you don't see a psychologist or counsellor when things are going well!

True dat! So where should the responsibility for adequate training lie? With the practitioner? What about the various institutions who develop the syllabuses, the membership bodies, public health and professional standards associations? I believe without firm commitment and big changes from the top we are doomed to keep making the same mistakes all over again.

> I don't necessarily think the DSM (Diagnostic and Statistical Manual of Mental Disorders) does have problems, I think the problem is actually connecting psychotherapy training institutions and psychological establishments who are developing criteria for diagnostics. They are not the same organizations, they're two separate kinds of disciplines. – Samantha Stein (Yo Samdy Sam), author and YouTuber

In Ali Cunningham Abbott's (2019) book on counselling adults with autism – personally sent to me all the way from the States by the author to help with my research (thanks, Ali!) – she describes how the worlds of psychotherapy and psychology have historically been kept apart (echoing Sam's comments that they are in fact different disciplines) and highlights that empowerment counselling is an important intervention to help neurodivergent individuals develop skills, self-awareness, realistic optimism, social belonging and advocacy.

> I have yet to have an ASD client not express treatment or medical trauma. They tend to be confused about who they are because they feel like an alien and no diagnosis given has ever made sense. It comes down to NT therapists believing they are always right without asking questions/clarifying/

using client terminology due to the educational system in the US telling clinicians they are the expert and there to fix the client. – therapist Michelle Hunt

A FRIGHTENING PICTURE

According to the NHS England (2022), the number of autistic people in inpatient facilities was a staggering 58%, which I suspect should be higher still, given that so many of us fly under the radar. The National Autistic Society (2022) also reports that 90% of autistic people held in hospitals are put there using the Mental Health Act 1983, with 'The Guardian' newspaper publishing a story (Pidd 2022) on how a 14-year-old autistic girl was unlawfully detained and subjected to a harrowing ordeal which judge Mr. Justice MacDonald described as 'brutal and abusive'.

Sadly I notice these stories are becoming more and more frequent, which begs the question: What the hell is going on at the point of psychiatric evaluation and why aren't clinicians spotting the signs? At the time of writing the UK Government has recently published a draft bill which should theoretically stop autistic individuals being wrongly detained by acknowledging that autism is **not** a mental health condition and ensuring that a range of support services are made available so that we don't get to crisis point in the first place. I'm not too embarrassed to admit this but if anyone were to ever see me in the middle of a serious meltdown I'm fairly sure it could be mistaken for a psychotic breakdown. Meltdowns can and will happen, and it is down to us to identify the triggers, reduce our overall stress and develop personalized coping strategies.

'Whilst distressing to hear about, I don't actually think my own situation is that unusual. Back in 2013 I was sectioned for being suicidal and kept on a ward where the lights and noise constantly triggered my fight or flight response. Feeling so trapped and not believed only made me angrier, and I overheard the staff talking about me as if I needed teaching a lesson. I was highly medicated on a variety of antipsychotics and antidepressants, which only made me worse, and it took years to come off everything. I'm sure services can provide a lot of help for some people but for me as an undiagnosed autistic, I came out traumatized, hooked on drugs and worse than I went in. I still felt suicidal and depressed, I just learned to hide it.'

'Looking back I realize that actually all of my experiences in counselling have been a kind of conversion therapy, trying to get me to blend in more with the neurotypical world. I know that I have to live in this world and that you wouldn't only insist on speaking your own language if you went to a foreign country, but way too many therapists have avoided what I wanted to work on and instead made me feel embarrassed that my tone wasn't right, or that I avoided making eye-contact, or that I was moving too much when I should be sitting still. I felt like I was constantly being corrected like some disobedient puppy in doggy boot camp.'

WHY ARE WE BEING MISDIAGNOSED?

To find out more I spoke to Debbie Palmer – an autistic specialist speech and language therapist, diagnostic clinician and neurodevelopmental specialist. She explains:

I think there are several factors which contribute to neurodivergent individuals receiving inaccurate diagnoses and feeling that they need to 'jump through hoops within the diagnostic process', including the need for individuals to mask their differences in an attempt to fit in within society, the history and continuation of the misogynistic and victim blaming culture of psychology and mental health services, the subconscious bias of some diagnostic clinicians, and the limitations of the current autism diagnostic tools.

As with all mental health assessments we are assessed on our observational behaviours – there are no blood tests or brain scans that can support the process – and we are completely reliant on the professional in front of us and their knowledge and understanding. Although the culture has changed slightly within the profession, there is still prejudice and judgement placed on females. Within large organizations it is harder to change the narrative, culture and practices, and often professionals who are knowledgeable (neurodivergent themselves and/or agree with the equality of different neurotypes) are silenced and ignored.

The other factor of misdiagnoses are the limitations of the autism diagnostic tools which are created and standardized against the general population. They are only as good as the clinicians using them, and assessments such as the ADI-r and the ADOS-2 (although considered the Gold Standard of diagnostic tools) are simply not sensitive enough to recognize masking behaviours and some autistic experiences. It takes a highly skilled professional to use the tool as a tool, and not as a conclusive document – it must be used as qualitative and not just quantitative data.

Many professionals decide on a negative outcome from one piece of data or single observation – 'they made eye-contact', 'they had a friend at primary school', 'they enjoy comedy', 'they like going to pubs', and so on.

For a lot of autistic and neurodivergent people this level of judgement is something we have experienced our whole lives and we often continue in mental health services with no real understanding of ourselves, suffering in silence and away from public view. For improvements in diagnostics and mental health services, we need a cultural change. We need to hear autistic voices and approach neurodiversity with an open, honest, accepting view that every neurotype is equal and important within the human species. We need to move away from the medical model.

I would say that due to the high emotional sensitivity many of us experience, it is all too easy for clinicians to make lazy assumptions and label us with borderline personality disorder. It may be difficult for us to pinpoint the sources of our distress and therefore look from the outside that we're having some kind of disproportionate tantrum or are just a difficult person.

I once read an international best-seller called 'Don't Sweat the Small Stuff (and It's All Small Stuff)' by Richard Carson, which encourages us to let go, be more patient and forget about imperfections. Whilst Richard's book was obviously designed to help people, for me it had the complete opposite effect and only made me feel there was something wrong with me.

Why was I getting so upset by there not being enough sugar in my tea, having a hair stuck down my jumper, my books being all higgledy-piggledy, getting a wet sock from standing on the bath-room mat, having to do the dishes without rubber gloves (eeeww!), the sound of my cat licking itself (dear God!), having my plans changed at the last minute, or not getting a text back from some-one (what does it mean?! Do they hate me?!). I have become an expert in hiding my hurt feelings from others owing to the fact that I have been called spoilt and dramatic more times than I care to repeat. Therapist Eleanor Yarisse also discussed the inherent prob-lems with mental health assessments particularly BPD explaining,

> Mental health issues are diagnosed by symptoms, not cause, so it would not technically be incorrect to diagnose someone with say, BPD, even if the underlying issue is undiagnosed autism, as long as they meet criteria. I think this is a big issue in the mental health field, but unfortunately that is how it is. When I have clients who may be autistic and also meet criteria for BPD, I keep in mind that personality disorders are the result of trauma, and that a person who has symptoms of BPD requires thoughtful care because they are by defini-tion high-risk. It seems illogical that autism and personality disorders require such different processes to get diagnosed.

Author and YouTuber Samantha Stein (Yo Samdy Sam) described how in her opinion clinicians tend to view autism as a checklist of traits. She believes the variations in neurodivergence could be better imagined as a series of constellations. She explains:

> Rather than list every star in the sky, I think we're more like constellations. You see, I'm not a unique special star, there are a lot of late-diagnosed women like me who are

highly educated and reasonably neurotic! That's us. We are
that constellation. We share many stars with other autistic
constellations but we are actually quite different. However
once you see the patterns, you can start to kind of create
more of a framework for it.

I absolutely agree with Samantha and can't help thinking there's
a need for a book on autistic archetypes, much in the same way
there is a dusty book on my shelf caricaturing different music lovers
(the indie kid, the rock chick, the folky, the raver). Maybe I'll write
it myself when I get my breath back from finishing this one...

MASKING

If you don't already know what autistic masking is – although I
think it's pretty fair to say you will since 94% of us do it at some
time or other (Sedgewick, Hull and Ellis 2022) – it is a conscious or
unconscious way of behaving which conceals the fact we're autistic.
Examples of this might include:

- Hiding self-soothing stimming behaviours
- Squashing down our emotions
- Forcing ourselves to have eye-contact
- Avoiding talking about our particular special interests
- Remembering pre-prepared scripts to help conversation
  flow
- Monitoring your own speech (volume/tone)
- Inhibiting our natural style of communication (blunt,
  direct, honest)
- Adapting facial expressions and body language (do I seem
  normal?!)

- Hiding sensory discomfort (like when the noise of a passing motorbike rips your spleen open but you pretend everything is fine and dandy)
- Pretending to care about socially accepted ideals
- Hiding your true opinions and feelings

...the list is endless and includes anything else you can think of which entails supressing our authenticity to fit in with neuronormative values. To my mind hiding anxiety and social confusion are also a type of masking, and I know from experience just how bloody exhausting it is. Sometimes the most confident, chatty, gregarious social butterfly is actually a highly introverted autistic person quietly dying inside and counting down the clock until it's time to leave the party (tick tick tick goes the social battery).

I am fully aware that, to be approved of, my own maladaptive coping strategy involves being a super-listener to everyone else to shift the focus off of me since I get a bit tongue-tied in conversation. I conceal my crippling internal discomfort (anxiety, muscle cramps, racing heart, blank mind) by 'powering through' and offset this by keeping my social interactions to a minimum.

Often on social media I will see people encouraging us to 'Take off the mask!' as if we're Tori Kelly about to whip off a sexy seahorse outfit, but the truth is, it really isn't that simple. If you aren't diagnosed until well into adulthood there is a good chance that your unconscious coping strategies to evade detection have intermingled with your personality to such a degree that you can't easily switch off this knee-jerk autopilot safety-seeking behaviour.

As a child I remember my mum demanding I sit still on the sofa and getting shouted at for jiggling my legs (which felt calming to me but clearly annoying to her). Nowadays I cannot sit on a sofa for any extended period of time (say watching a film) without feeling like I'm going to explode. It's as if my jiggly legs got internalized and now they just violently vibrate where no one can see.

The real difficulty for the Gandalf gatekeepers of autism assessments ('You shall not paaaaass!') is that so many of us are just too good at masking and slip through the net. We give Oscar-worthy performances on a daily basis, and it's often only later in the privacy of our own homes that the wheels fall off when we unexpectedly run out of loo roll.

When I was little I was constantly having meltdowns and shutdowns, but it was always attributed to my being 'overly tired' or 'misbehaving'. My family would accuse me of 'acting up', insisting that because my problematic behaviour didn't manifest around everyone I must have some degree of control over it. You tend to take things literally when you're autistic (and ikkle) and such comments made me grow up with a belief that I was a bad person and deeply manipulative underneath. It breaks my heart to think that actually I was just surrounded by a bunch of caregivers projecting their shadow characteristics onto me. Even now I have to talk myself out of this toxic logic. Sometimes in the middle of a meltdown – despite being flooded with emotional pain – I will still hear that negative critical voice in my head, 'You're such a drama queen, stop acting like a child and grow up.'

Autistic shame is a feeling many of us experience, sometimes not even knowing where it comes from, and we carry with us a rotten core belief that being authentically ourselves is unpleasant for other people and that to be liked we must hide aspects of ourselves. The sad reality is that, if we do not learn to recognize and remove (or at least partially remove) the mask, the Kate Winslets and Leonardo DiCaprios amongst us will plummet head first into a bucket load of mental health issues, suicidal thoughts (or worse), severe burnout, ill health, increased autistic symptoms (such as sensory sensitivities and emotional dysregulation) or experience a significant identity crisis. And there we are again, sat in the doctor's chair as they see only the presenting symptoms, not the underlying cause, leading us right back to feeling that **we** must be the problem.

'My psychologist only had experience with children with very obvious traits and almost laughed me out of the consultation. Fortunately my husband was with me and was able to remain composed (given that my brain had shutdown and I'd lost the ability to advocate for myself) and explained that I had been masking for 50 years, so it shouldn't come as a surprise that I presented as "normal". The psychologist seemed to take what he said on board, but without him being there, it would be a different story now.'

Aside from masking, poor quality training, stereotypes, sexism, generalizations and myths, another major factor to consider in missed diagnoses is racial and ethnic discrimination and invalidation. Recent research carried out by Malone et al. (2022) found a scholarly neglect of Black autistic adults and explores the importance of thoughtful and intentional inclusion. Christin Fontes, a Licensed Professional Counselor, shares her deeply moving feelings on the topic:

We owe Black girls better. I think of all the suicidal days. I think of all of the overmedicated days. I think of all of the days where I had the intrinsic knowing – knowing that I wasn't what they said I was, but being powerless to do anything other than trusting my caretakers and educators. My heart breaks for all the other Christins that ran out of time.

> That gave in to the suicidal thoughts. That weren't listened to. That ended up in graves.

Christin makes a hugely important point in describing her experience of racism and healthcare disparities, clearly showing how institutionalized invalidation and medical ignorance leads to trauma, which as we will see in the following chapter is already a serious and potentially deadly problem for autistic individuals.

SUMMARY

The majority of people are only familiar with a certain (often visible) presentation of autism largely due to the media and historical stereotypes resulting in widespread under-diagnosis.

- Autism is a neurological difference (a separate neurotype), not a mental health issue. It affects everyone differently and no two autistic people are alike, even if they share profile similarities.

- Before being correctly diagnosed most autistic people will have been incorrectly labelled with a psychiatric disorder, which in many instances may be secondary to autism – a consequence of being undiagnosed, suppression of self, inauthenticity or maladaptive coping strategies.

- Misdiagnosis arises from a number of factors including poor or non-existent training, outdated medical knowledge and assumptions, clinicians not understanding the complexity of masking, institutionalized sexism and racism, sexual orientation and cultural discrimination, and standardized tests not being sophisticated enough to collect illuminating data.

Chapter 2

TRAUMA

'It's like... the aisles of the supermarket get **inside** my head, do you know what I mean? All the lights and sounds, it flips me out, makes me dizzy. All those rows of identical products beaming into my skull under flickering lights. The chatter, the metal trolley noises and bloody till beeps – eeesh! It's like needles in my brain, it's actually very painful. I used to wear earmuffs as a little girl, that helped a bit I guess. But probably not the best look for me now.'

'You're describing your hyper-vigilance and anxiety, yes?' said Veronica, sniffing violently through her left nostril.

'Well, I guess so... it's just that... well... I've been in and out of therapy for about ten years now and nothing seems to be **really** working all that well. I'm not actually getting any... better.'

'Stephanie...' (I hate it when she uses my name in full, I've been a Steph all my life and asked her repeatedly not to call me Stephanie.) 'It's **my** job as **your** therapist to be honest, and I believe you're not getting any better because you're avoiding the material you **need** to be looking at.'

I feel totally puzzled by her observation as I have never been anything but truthful in our sessions. It wouldn't serve me to avoid anything at these extortionate prices. And besides that's

just not my style (in fact since I was tiny the world has instructed me to be **less honest** about what I'm thinking and feeling –
apparently most people dislike the truth and prefer a lukewarm
bowl of beat-around-the-bush word-soup.) Each week I come
prepared with another exciting chapter in the history of Steph
Jones in the hope that when she has gathered all the material
something new and shiny will leap out and help me make sense
of my life. I can't even describe it fully at this stage, on paper I'm
doing well (house, tick, car, tick, career, tick, relationship, tick),
but everything just seems so frickin' hard.

When I was a teenager my mum felt it was important for me to
start 'challenging my shyness' by doing more and more things
like ordering for myself in a restaurant, which felt like a truly
terrifying experience. I remember saying to Mum, 'What if I
can't remember what to ask for?' and she would look at me as
if that was the most ridiculous thing she'd ever heard. Even now,
ordering a cheeseburger at McDonald's feels like an impossible
game of sudoku (thank heavens for self-service machines…). I'm
always ready with my opening lines (which I silently repeat to
myself as I stand in the queue), but there will always be some
advanced quantum physics-esque follow-up questions I am
ill-prepared for which no doubt makes me look a bit simple. It's like other people can just manage the back-and-forth
of everyday conversation without giving it any thought, but
for me it seems like I'm living in an improvised comedy sketch.

'I've spoken to my therapy supervisor about our sessions and
she thinks I'm a classic case of complex PTSD. I've started reading up on the symptoms and I'm inclined to agree with her, I
definitely tick all the boxes.'

Veronica narrows her crinkly eyes at me, which feels like she has
just poured a truck load of molten metal into my abdomen.

I have said the wrong thing. Again. I am often unclear about non-verbal inference (why can't people just say what they mean?!) but have suspected for a while she thinks I have borderline personality disorder (BPD). It's not so much that I'm opposed to a diagnosis of BPD in the slightest (stigma can get in the bin as far as I'm concerned), only it feels untruthful, and being clear and straight is very important to me. Anything else causes so much mess in my head that I don't know how to tidy it up.

'Veronica, I'm really uncertain about what you're getting at. What do **you** think I'm dealing with? Are you suggesting I have BPD?'

Veronica shrugs her slender shoulders in a slightly passive-aggressive manner, raises her eyebrows and takes an elongated breath, which causes her to levitate from her chair. She says nothing. The silence is deafening.

'But... my supervisor doesn't think that **is** the case and she's worked with me for years now. Plus, I don't like conflict and never fall out with anyone, and I'm not afraid of being left on my own – in fact I prefer it!'

More radio silence. I continue with listing my own self-reflections, not to avoid, deny or deflect any truth but to really **find the truth**. I need to understand what the hell is wrong with me because that is the only way I will be fixed. 'I don't miss people, I don't ever feel "empty" and I don't have an inconsistent sense of identity – in fact I am boringly predictable in routine, behaviour, and appearance, having not changed my wardrobe or hair-do since 1997.'

'Perhaps you don't miss people because you've been so hurt in the past and keep others at arm's length. Maybe that's happening in our relationship too.'

I pause for a moment to collect my thoughts and recalculate my algorithm, she is the expert after all. I **do** have a kind of all-or-nothing thinking pattern which seems to flop around willy-nilly with the phases of the moon (one month wanting the same sandwich every single day but then out of nowhere never wanting to see a sandwich again as long as I live). I **do** have occasional angry outbursts – never with other people but certainly with inanimate household objects, like noisy teaspoons which accidentally crash onto the floor. And I **do** have a history of unstable relationships. But is that my fault? I thought they were all just wankers.

'I think it's best we keep private therapy conversations to ourselves, Stephanie. Involving others in our discussions only adds confusion,' said Veronica, her thin lips revealing what appears to be a micro-snarl. 'We don't want to... muddy the water.'

Although words are incredibly important to me (some might even call me pedantic) I navigate through life using a kind of sixth sense animal instinct – intuition, patterns and energies are all I need to work out a person's intentions. I have an uncanny knack for cold reading others and don't get why people say things like 'Ted seems lovely, doesn't he?' when it's blatantly obvious that Mr. Bundy is a deranged serial killer.

Our time is up and I leave the room feeling dazed and confused. Therapy never leaves me feeling contented or as though I understand myself a little deeper, it's more like a quicksand forcing me to let go of everything I **know** to be true and replacing it with the 'healthy' thoughts of someone else. I get into my car and sob uncontrollably. Little do I know at the time but I am in a dangerously traumatic and gaslighting relationship with my therapist. I am deep in the heart of radicalization.

WHAT IS TRAUMA ANYWAY?

As an often binary thinking creature who likes to put things in nice, neat little boxes I spent a large amount of my time asking myself the question I think we all fall into at some point – Is the way I am down to trauma or autism?

There are two schools of thought around what constitutes psychological trauma depending on who you're talking to, which we might affectionately refer to as Big-T and Little-T trauma. Whilst there are some professionals who only consider trauma to be valid if an experience was actually life-threatening (that's your Big-T trauma, things like war, being attacked or having a terrible car accident), the word trauma itself comes from the Greek word for 'wound', which to my mind must surely incorporate emotional distress and not just purely physical danger. Little-T traumas tend to include things like relational abuse (bullying, interpersonal exploitation or harassment), a divorce, job loss, money worries and grief – anything that may not be thought of as life-threatening but may certainly be life-changing.

In psychological circles we are starting to shift our way of thinking about a person's trauma history so that it's less about 'what's wrong with someone' and more about 'what's happened to them'. Unlike physical and emotional abuse where something tangible has happened to us, neglect is considered to be an abuse by omission, whereby our needs (not just the physical but other emotional aspects such as security, love, consistency, empathy, safety, constructive feedback) go unmet, typically at the hands of a caregiver or institution. However, if we think about the very nature of being autistic in a society which largely holds negative views about the condition, one might argue that the social order at large is failing our neurodivergent population's most basic psychological needs for acceptance, belonging, appreciation and respect.

The message that somehow our needs aren't that important often starts early on – I recall my own mother's stories that I was a 'frustrating colicky baby' (colic is where a baby cries a lot and no one quite knows why). I can still remember her energetic annoyance with me. In her spare time she would knit me fluffy woollen jumpers, which only left me crying (being unable to communicate my sensory distress at the fabric). I was guilt-tripped into eating foods I didn't like the texture of (because there are 'children starving in Africa') and was regularly told off for being too fussy and demanding.

I hold a deeply unhappy memory of my childhood in which I was stealth listening into a conversation Mum was having with her best friend (both very drunk). 'She's just too much for me, I'm sick of it, I can't cope, I wish she would just go and live with her dad!' The takeaway for that little eight-year-old girl was that she was unlovable, unwanted and would only get her needs met through dogged compliance, being perfect and repressing her innate 'weirdness'.

The attachment wounds I received have taken many years to work through, but I suspect my neurodivergent story is far from exceptional. Of course this is nobody's fault and we certainly do not need to be wagging blameful fingers at well-meaning nurturing parents doing their very best to raise their undiagnosed infant, but it is important to think about the broader implications of living in a world not attuned to our human experience. But what actually **is** trauma? Is it just an unpleasant memory? How do we get rid of it? And how can we fathom which parts of us are struggling due to past painful experiences and which are down to the challenges we face as neurodivergent people?

Trauma in a nutshell

To understand things a bit better I met up with Dr. Naomi Fisher who is an independent clinical psychologist, author and EMDR consultant who specializes in trauma, autism and alternative approaches to education. Naomi explains:

When something happens to us there are two ways it can be remembered in our brains. The way that we remember day-to-day things is that they get stored in our hippocampus, which is a bit like a filing cabinet with a date tag attached. Something that happened ten years ago feels further away than something that happened yesterday. We can retrieve those memories from the hippocampus, but when we do it doesn't feel like they're happening again. They are just memories.

Then we've got our amygdala which is where memories are stored at a time of high arousal (when we feel frightened or under threat). And if the hippocampus is like a filing cabinet, the amygdala is the chaos cupboard under the stairs! It's like we screw up the memories, shove them in there, slam the door and hope for the best. Because everything is thrown in together we might have no cohesive narrative – sensations and emotions may seem fragmented and not make much sense, and the lack of a date stamp means that when we remember things it feels like we're right back in that place, like it's happening again. In addition, the amygdala is used to inform our brain's perception of danger – it is the alarm system in the brain – the bit that can trigger off our survival responses (fight, flight, freeze and fawn responses), using our memories as ways to hone our perception of danger. It looks for indications in our environment that we might be in danger and uses our memories to inform that.

Blimey! So not only is the chaos cupboard under the stairs jumbling everything up but it actually informs part of our navigation system through life? One of the big problems we have in Western medical culture is that somewhere along the way, the mind and the body became separate entities. Despite the fact that we are one system sharing the same hormonal, immune, endocrine and nervous systems, all too often trauma is perceived as an event (or series of events) that gives rise to a body-based medical problem to treat. In my opinion, human emotions have become over-medicalized, and I cannot tell you how many self-diagnosed 'depressed' people I've met who were actually just experiencing feelings of sadness entirely relative to an upsetting experience, as if having negative emotions is wrong.

Naomi's explanation reminds me that unhealed trauma undoubtedly shapes who we are in the world. If we don't feel safe, we cannot grow and we become limited in authentic expression. I personally favour the biopsychosocial approach to any therapeutic practice and firmly believe that if we are to compassionately tame our hyper-reactive nervous systems, we must tackle it from all angles. We need to be not only thinking or talking about the traumatic event, but also recognizing that our environment shapes who we are too. What good is going to therapy and rehashing painful events if our lives are unsuitable in terms of being neurodivergent-friendly?

ARE AUTISTIC PEOPLE BIOLOGICALLY AT GREATER RISK FOR TRAUMA?

It's a sad but true reality that trauma appears to be a constant in the life of autistic people, resulting from:

- feeling generally misunderstood
- experiencing ableism
- loneliness
- having to endure painful sensory experiences that others don't understand
- issues around unemployment (e.g. being incredibly over-qualified but flunking interviews due to social struggles)
- bullying
- a chronic state of stress, which often causes secondary physical and emotional health problems.

Research suggests that autistic adults are four times more likely to be diagnosed with PTSD than the general population (Lobregt-van Buuren, Hoekert and Sizoo 2021), and I would argue that this figure is likely to be much higher when we take into account the narrow definition of trauma according to the fifth edition of the 'Diagnostic and Statistical Manual of Mental Disorders' (American Psychiatric Association 2013) as 'actual or threatened death, serious injury, or sexual violence'.

Whilst there doesn't appear to be any conclusive evidence (yet!) there are a number of theories which suggests that autistic individuals are more susceptible to PTSD from a neurological and genetic vulnerability position. This makes complete sense if you consider how we are often more sensitive to stimuli (both internal and external).

One study I found interesting was a 2019 piece of research exploring reduced heart rate variability (HRV) in adults with autism spectrum disorder (Thapa et al. 2019). They suggested that compared to neurotypical individuals our autonomic nervous system may find it more challenging to deal with stress (think of it like an inflexible system which struggles to return to baseline functionality after being shaken up). An elevated resting heart rate will naturally mean a heightened state of arousal, and for many of us we talk about never feeling at ease in our bodies. Naturally that is going to make the entire world seem difficult to deal with. So how could anyone manage the simplest of interactions when our stress levels are through the roof?!

The important nerve which controls HRV is called the vagus nerve and is the main control bit for our parasympathetic nervous systems and, important to note, is totally out of conscious operation. (We cannot think ourselves calm any more than we can think our digestive system into not being constipated!) Initial research shows that this cranial nerve may be slightly different in autistic people, which I expect is why certain relaxation techniques and therapies may fall short. Although studies are in their infancy, some researchers believe that stimulation of the vagus nerve may be a beneficial 'treatment' for neurodivergent people (Engineer, Hayes and Kilgard 2017). But again, what is it we're trying to treat? I'm not ill the last time I checked but could certainly do with some decent inner peace!

When I'm working with a client it's sometimes helpful to describe this as having challenges in metabolizing stress, much in the same way you'd find it hard to break down alcohol if your liver wasn't working properly. It kind of doesn't matter if the actual stressor is removed, it will still take a longer period to digest the stress hormones. Because mind over matter won't sober you up either!.

Other researchers believe that the amygdala itself is enlarged in people with autism spectrum disorder, but for me this feels like a bit of a chicken and egg situation (did stress and sensory overload enlarge it or is it just part of our make-up?). The truth is right now, we're not quite sure. For what it's worth I think you will be hard pushed to find a non-traumatized autistic person here on planet Earth, and I believe it's important that clinicians have a decent understanding of both neurodiversity and trauma if they are to do due diligence in their work. Because let's be honest, Veronica isn't doing very well right now, explaining my entire life away through her trauma-goggles and totally oblivious to the seven-foot pink dancing elephant in the room waving a ruddy flag that says 'This person is clearly autistic'.

WHAT ABOUT ADDITIONAL RISKS?

Professor Tony Attwood describes how autistic individuals often experience a lot more trauma or abuse in all forms and believes that difficulties in understanding people's motives can often find us being the target of ill-intentioned folk and wondering 'Why me?'. Without being able to accurately understand why someone would behave so negatively towards us, we may struggle to find closure, trapping us into traumatic rumination and unable to process the feelings. One client I worked with remarked:

> What I find difficult to deal with is understanding how some people can be so cruel and just lie. I hold fairness, justice and morality so close to my heart that I just don't get people with darker natures. Like, my ex seemed to enjoy power games and hurting me, and I've had family members exclude me and not make the effort. I'd never do that. I can't get rid of the thoughts, they just go around and around in my

head like a horrible fairground ride. I can't move on because
I can't figure it out.

Tony describes how a lot of his work is around educating autistic
people on the psychology of predators to make sense of their experiences. He also explains how the autistic tendency to engage in
repetitive behaviours (which can most certainly include thinking)
means that memory wounds become deeper over time, effectively
never healing and becoming a new (false) self-belief. In his clinic he
helps clients to see a more accurate view of reality and to broaden
that which we are blocking out due to cognitive bias (where we
only notice or believe things which supports our world view).

It can often feel hard for us not to take things personally when
someone insults or criticizes us, especially since words can feel so
literal. If you've been repeatedly told you're 'weird' enough times
over the course of your life, it's extremely tough to set that aside
and simply recognize that actually, at times, some people just suck.
Everyone has an opinion on everything, it doesn't mean it's the
universal truth. Tony believes that much of the trauma work we
need to undertake is around reframing and challenging those negative self-beliefs based upon lifelong rejections, bullying, teasing
and humiliation. And that we need to learn to seek out reliable
compliments and support from those without a negative agenda.

COMPLEX POST-TRAUMATIC
STRESS DISORDER (CPTSD)

I once had a wonderful therapist who set me some homework to
write down all the traumas I wanted to work on. There were 50 (all
organized into colour-coded sections and sub-sections, of course).

In the following session he asked which ones were causing me the most concerns – flashbacks, nightmares, avoiding situations, panic attacks, intrusive thoughts – but when I really thought about it none of them were. 'So these are just stressful memories to you?' he asked. But to be honest I had just decided that these must be the significant inflection points at the heart of my challenges. You could probably even boil it down to a few words: The world is a scary place and people are dangerous.

Neurodivergent therapist James Barrott describes this kind of autistic predicament as

> more one of the world often having been corrosive – experiencing the sum of many different smaller incidents over many years, which results in a default position of not finding the world supportive.

Therapist Shanna Kramer expresses how being punished for our differences is a common theme she sees in her work stating how:

> Not having needs met, being ridiculed, isolated, and meant to feel stupid or inadequate repeatedly over the course of their childhood or lifespan becomes a recipe for CPTSD.

In basic terms we can distinguish typical post-traumatic stress disorder (PTSD) from complex post-traumatic stress disorder (CPTSD) as PTSD being caused by a single event and CPTSD caused by a collection of emotional wounds (usually interpersonal in nature). You may also hear the term 'developmental trauma' (which is often used interchangeably with CPTSD but can also mean the pre-cursor to adult CPSTD), which describes how without sufficient early care, children will not 'wire together' properly. You can see how this can really throw a spanner in the works when trying to assess for autism. Perhaps if we stopped perceiving ASD through the medical lens of deficit and symptoms we might move away from the confusing overlaps.

Nowadays when I'm working with a client who suspects they're autistic I'm listening out for alternative clues, such as:

- the ability to hyper-focus
- a good memory
- attention to detail
- pattern recognition
- speaking honestly
- being non-judgemental
- having deep and intense passions
- having superhero-like senses.

In his ground-breaking work 'Complex PTSD: From Surviving to Thriving' (a must for anyone looking for a clear recovery roadmap) author and psychotherapist Pete Walker (2013) talks about something called 'emotional flashbacks' in which an old, familiar and unprocessed traumatic emotion gets re-activated in the here and now. Unlike the wounded veteran returning home from war and having a full-on panic attack at the sound of a passenger jet flying overhead, complex PTSD triggers can feel like they come out of nowhere and it may take a great deal of self-reflection to recognize the origins of the flashback. But are we having unidentified flying flashbacks or are we actually having an autistic meltdown due to sensory overload?

'I spent a year in therapy trying to work through my "emotional flashbacks" before I was diagnosed with autism. Every time my housemate would get excited about something I would have this urge to really punch him in the face, which made no sense at all! My therapist convinced me I must be being triggered by "something", and we went on for weeks and weeks about my parents and any rows they had. In hindsight, it was a total waste of time. I now realize that my housemate was just really being loud and overwhelming me. I nearly lost a good mate over that!'

Unfortunately since our histories and experiences are as unique as we are, we will only reach our own truth through a journey of deep self-reflection and introspection. From the table below can you start to see what might be showing up as trauma in your life and what might be down to your own autistic profile (or both)?

Complex PTSD	Autistic Spectrum Disorders
Feelings of guilt	Not inherent parts of an ASD diagnosis although may have negative self-image due to a lifetime of feeling different and not knowing why
Feelings of shame	
Feelings of worthlessness	
Problems controlling emotions	Emotional dysregulation due to unsuitable or overwhelming environments (meltdowns/shutdowns)
Hyper-vigilance	Hyper-sensitivity
Difficulties connecting with others due to lack of trust	Difficulties with social communication issues due to processing differences
Difficulties keeping relationships	Difficulties with social reciprocity and understanding neurotypical expectations, resulting in challenges in maintaining friends

Re-experiencing of traumatic events	Repetitive thinking such as rumination, and inability to switch off thoughts without distractions
Avoidance of things reminding you of the abuse/trauma	Preference for being alone or spending limited time with others due to small social battery (masking fatigue)
Not being able to remember parts of the trauma	Struggles with executive dysfunction and working memory
Dissociation	Autistic shutdown or zoning out due to exceeding mental capacity (but sometimes reported as a pleasurable sensory break or empty mind)
Nightmares	Difficulties sleeping in general, and higher stress response on a daily basis resulting in low-grade sleep

It is perhaps also worth noting that the psychiatric professions have sought to keep complex PTSD out of the 'Diagnostic and Statistical Manual of Mental Disorders' (despite its recognition by the World Health Organization's International Classification of Diseases) with Pete Walker (2013) sharing a remark of the renowned traumatologist John Briere that if it were to be included it would reduce it to the size of the average pamphlet!

WHO GETS TO DECIDE WHAT IS TRAUMATIC FOR US?

One of the difficulties of neurotypical diagnostic frameworks is that they do not take into consideration **how** autistic people experience the world. When my mother died one Friday evening back in 2012 everyone around me spoke about how traumatic this must be for me. Of course I was upset, but in my mind I was more concerned that I had a job interview arranged for the Monday morning. Being unemployed, skint and sleeping on my friend's sofa at the time, I took the pragmatic approach that I must attend and cracked on with my preparation (essentially crafting scripts I could rehearse to appear normal under pressure).

I remember hearing an aunt talking about me in the kitchen shortly after Mum's funeral, 'Poor thing is in shock, it'll hit her later, she's just keeping herself busy.' None of that was true, and I felt really annoyed that anyone would dare to imply that they knew my feelings better than I did.

I processed my grief in a more cognitive way (turning it into a special interest project in hindsight), learning all about alcoholism and how it affects the organs, exploring cultural beliefs around death and immersing myself in spiritual teachings. I'm certainly not a person devoid of emotion (you could argue I have too much!), yet unacquainted therapists would still decide that I was repressing, suppressing or minimizing my own experiences. Ironically, being accused of lying when I'm permanently wearing the inside out **does** feel deeply traumatic to me.

> 'I quit my well-paid job in advertising after only a year much to the dismay of my family. I'd worked so hard to get there and it wasn't the job I had a problem with, it was the endless streams of people milling around the open-plan office, the radio being on all the time, not having enough space to think... Initially I was signed off with "stress" but it's only now I understand that the whole experience was deeply traumatic. But try telling the doctor that you want to be formally assessed for PTSD because work has the radio on all the time and your colleagues are too friendly.'

Many of the things that feel traumatic to **us** are often based around:

- sensory issues (noise, lights, pungent smells, textures, temperature, the vibe of an environment, other people's energy)
- small or big unexpected changes
- disruptions to plans and routines
- not having enough space to mentally switch tasks or feel adequately prepared
- masking to fit in socially
- daily demands and activities we don't see the point in.

For those of us who have pathological demand avoidance as part of our profile, this last point can be especially traumatic. You wouldn't expect a goldfish to thrive living in a bag of sand, yet that's kind of what we go through 24/7 without manageable adjustments to make things more tolerable.

OTHER REASONS STRESS AND TRAUMA ARE HARD TO OVERCOME WITH AUTISM

- We may hyper-focus on a problem in an unsuccessful attempt to rationalize it (solving the unsolvable).
- We may be unable to break out of rumination/ perseverance, and/or have rigid thinking styles, such as all or nothing/catastrophizing.
- We may misinterpret our feelings and internal sensations.
- We may not have adequate support systems in place to discuss things bothering us (not having a second pair of eyes to look at a situation differently or share the load).
- Injustice and unfairness feels morally wrong to us.
- We may avoid conflict because we lack social skills and confidence, struggle to find the right words, or feel so overstimulated during a negative interaction that we cannot stay present (freeze, panic, stutter, get jumbled up).

- We might fear upsetting someone with our words or feelings (even if they're being nasty idiots to us!).
- We may doubt our perception (particularly if an abusive person is passive-aggressive and their toxic behaviour is less obvious to work out).
- We have been told our problems are no big deal by others so often that we wonder if our feelings are valid.
- We may be living with autistic burnout, further limiting our capacity to cope. (I cannot tell you how many clients I work with who whilst usually self-describing as 'bomb-proof in a crisis' go to pieces when they are going through a burnout. One client remarked, 'Even my cat meowing for its food can feel like I'm having a nervous breakdown as my insides shatter under the weight of responsibility.')

I sometimes feel a little frustrated (oh, okay then, absolutely livid!) when others assume our 'over-reactions' are something we should just be able to 'deal with' psychologically, despite the overwhelming evidence that it isn't possible with such a sensitive central nervous system. Being autistic isn't about having a weak character. If we could change our internal distress response, of course we would all do it. But we can't. Over the course of my life I became a master in hiding how painful things are just to avoid causing offence to someone else. It truly sucked.

SILVER LININGS

Whilst sifting the lumps (is it autism, trauma or both?!) to my mind at least the goal is pretty much the same: to self-regulate. In Pete Walker's book (mentioned earlier) he has created a brilliant 13-step technique for managing PTSD flashbacks which I believe are totally transferable to dealing with an autistic meltdown (well, most of them anyway!) and has also made it free to access on his webpage if you wanted to have a look.[1]

One of the first things I do with my clients is to help them put together their own first-aid toolkit for the times when they are really struggling, as I know from experience that when I am in the middle of a meltdown remembering the things I need to do to calm down are just not available to me at any rational thinking level. I keep my own A4 toolkit pinned to my fridge, so at least I stand a chance of noticing it when I'm feeling all end-of-the-worldly. You might like to include specific instructions such as:

- eat your favourite snack
- try stimming
- take a soothing shower
- listen to a calming podcast
- watch a funny video (I have links to all manner of hilarious clips stored in my phone and adore drag queens Trixie and Katya – they should come on prescription)
- stroke a pet
- drink water
- be in nature
- make a duvet fort
- read particular quotes
- ensure your room is sensory friendly... and so on.

...whatever works, works. Some of these things may need to be planned out in advance, but I find just a gentle reminder of who I am and what I need has really helped me in my darkest meltdown hours. This too shall pass.

Whilst there are a good many caring and empathic people out

---

1   www.pete-walker.com/13StepsManageFlashbacks.htm

there, for the most part neurotypical people just don't get it (us) but only in the same way we don't get them. When I tell my neurotypical friends that I am stressed writing a paper for example, they will interpret that as though stress is some kind of thought process I just need to push through (like a state of mind). In reality what is happening for me is that forcing myself to do something I don't want to do is **physically painful**, as if all my organs and muscles are clenched up, my head hurts, I lose my vision, my breathing goes shallow and I get a searing pain in my stomach.

Essentially what is happening is that my body cannot cope with the demand, perceives a major threat, and floods me with epinephrine. Honestly it's unbearable and I am fully aware that over time if not correctly managed will result in serious physiological consequences. Their friendly advice to 'just take a break' doesn't help matters when things will still have to get done and only really serves to make me feel more misunderstood and not taken seriously.

Whilst not a book about autism, in his international best-seller 'The Body Keeps the Score' Bessel van der Kolk (2015) does a great job in breaking down the anatomy of the brain. He addresses the kinds of problems someone might face around focus, attention and concentration with executive dysfunction – definitely worth a read if you are interested in some of the nuts and bolts of trauma and general brain mechanical wizardry.

Now that we understand a little bit about trauma it's worth reflecting on just how inherently traumatic the world can feel simply by being autistic in a society which does not recognize, appreciate or accommodate those differences. However, although we now recognize what we're dealing with, how easy will it be for us to feel understood by our therapists if we're having an entirely different perception of the world? Let's explore the broader implications in the following chapter.

SUMMARY

- Trauma is less about what is wrong with a person than about what has happened to someone and how that interacts with an autistic operating system.
- Autistic people are statistically more likely to experience conditions such as post-traumatic stress disorder (PTSD) from a biological, psychological and neurological perspective as well as a social vulnerability.
- The very experience of being an autistic person in a neurotypical society can be traumatic. Multiple 'small' traumas compound in complex PTSD (due to sensory issues, communication differences, relational abuse, uncertainty, external pressure and demands).
- There are both similarities and differences in symptom presentation of complex PTSD and autism.

Chapter 3

DO YOU SEE
WHAT I SEE?

Sessions with Veronica are exhausting. She really doesn't seem all that interested in what I want to talk about and instead tries to turn everything back to **our** relationship. So that I don't feel lost in sessions (sometimes my mind can go a bit blank, especially if we're conversationally darting about all over the place) I like to take in my prep-notes for the week. She doesn't seem to like this though, and apparently it doesn't fit with free association. Only, if I don't have my notes I can very easily feel steamrollered into discussions that I don't really understand or find applicable to my situation. Veronica tells me I must 'stop controlling the therapy' which is another indicator of my desire to 'avoid intimacy'. I put my pen down and start to feel like the world's most overwhelmed waitress, trying to remember everybody's order and terrified of dropping the plates.

I describe how one of the things I find difficult to comprehend is why I seem to have such a small social battery. 'It's as though I can be having a lovely time with friends, or out for a meal, or a drink or whatever, and then suddenly there is this internal collapse where I am desperate to go home. In fact my friend Becks has nicknamed me Dexy! You know, out of Dexys Midnight Runners? The band from the 80s? Sang "Come on Eileen"...?'

Clearly my encyclopaedic knowledge of pop music is lost on her as without even acknowledging what I'd said she blurted, 'Now you describe how the **topics** of conversation you seem to have with your friends are largely around emotional processing – either yours, or their feelings, correct?'

I nod in agreement, sounds legit.

'It all sounds rather heavy and **deep**, doesn't it? Social chit-chat is supposed to be light, bouncy and invigorating. Time spent with others should be pleasurable, not draining.'

That makes sense, I guess... only I can't stand small talk and really enjoy honest and meaty discussions. 'So, are you suggesting that I'm sort of working on my leisure time, and that actually it's my friends that are draining me?'

'It's less about what I think, Stephanie, it's more about what **you** think.'

Only that doesn't feel truthful at all. I dive into my imagination and picture my closest friends in the room, all with their amazing quirky lifting energies and exciting stories. I don't find them draining at all, it's more like I feel overstimulated and fizzle out like a corner shop firework.

I then visualize Veronica at some ostentatious Friday night soirée, glass of champers in hand, fake laughs filling the drawing room, and a cacophony of intellectual opinions about culture, politics and history. My big nights usually consist of drinking too much prosecco, falling over, and waking up with a slice of bread stuck to my face. I don't think I've ever felt so judged in life as I do here in her office. It isn't only that we are like chalk and cheese in terms of personality, it's that she doesn't seem to understand anything I'm saying as I mean it. Her analysis is often so far off the mark but trying to steer her back on track only results in her stopping the car altogether until we travel in **her** direction.

'What are you feeling now?' she asks, as if I'm some lab rat in an experiment.

'Nothing, really,' I respond with total sincerity.

'No, you can't feel nothing. That's simply not possible. You must feel something in this moment. Do you mean that you feel stunned? Empty? Annoyed?'

'No, not at all.' I reply. 'I feel full inside – whole, complete. Just stillness, really. Nothingness. The big space within that's eternally quiet. It isn't happy or sad, it's a place of no mind, of no feeling.'

This time Veronica inhales the entire room through her nostrils. I swear to God one of the pictures flew off the wall.

'Stephanie, you can't be full of nothing. If you're not prepared to co-operate in sessions, we might have to work towards an ending. These absurd answers you provide are only wasting your own time. I believe that you shutdown your feelings because you don't want to face them. It's perhaps not a conscious thing, but you're avoiding them nonetheless.'

I can't stand that she keeps talking about unconscious feelings like it's her golden ticket to prove me wrong. Despite doing my absolute best, sticking with the process, being painfully honest, and more to the point **forcing** myself to engage with someone I don't even like on a weekly basis... I am getting nowhere. I close my eyes and start scratching my scalp with exploratory fingertips. I like doing this and feel there's nothing more satisfying than finding a bit in your hair and then flicking it away from under your fingernails.

'Veronica, I don't feel that you understand me at all well. Whenever I try to explain something it's like you strip it all down and make me sound like someone I'm not. Trust me I am working really hard but I just don't agree with your interpretations.'

At this point she smiles at me with huge beige teeth and begins to nod as if I have finally done the trick she's wanted me to do. It immediately twigs in my brain: she **wants** a confrontation. She **thinks** that I am transferring my 'unresolved feelings towards my mother' onto her and in that moment I realize I've been caught in a pointless game of cat and mouse for nearly six months. I came to therapy in need of sound advice yet her goal has always been to trap me in a corner of transference using deliberate antagonization.

Ever since I was little I've had this sense that I'm not quite seeing the world as most people do. I can only describe my experience as a kind of hyper-reality where sounds are louder and more defined, colours are brighter, patterns exist everywhere and details are microscopic. In my twenties I became more aware of this difference when some of my friends began experimenting with psychedelics. They would gasp in a kind of mystical awe when the formerly plain wallpaper would spontaneously become a living tapestry of smudges, bumps, flecks and shapes (i.e. how I see things usually).

Masses of research backs up our perceptual anecdotal accounts (Jones, Quigney and Huws 2003; Khalfa et al. 2004; MacLennan, O'Brien and Tavassoli 2021), and needless to say living with sensory issues can be a deeply distressing and painful experience.

Whilst many autistic people can struggle to interpret social cues and facial expressions, there are just as many who have an almost excruciating magnification of this. Many of the clients who come to me have spent a lifetime being told they're paranoid or 'reading into things' when truthfully they're just picking up on environmental data others don't notice – a bit like being a human NASA telescope.

'Before I knew I was on the spectrum I'd had a number of therapists decide my ability to see patterns, signs, interconnections and coincidences were actually signs of mental illness and magical thinking. I was strongly encouraged to ignore my intuitive observations for what they considered to be a more accurate view of reality. I don't want to say that autistic people live in a different kind of reality but, maybe we do. Not an imaginary one by any means but one more similar to how animals experience things? Or babies before they get conditioned? Who knows? I just know that my time in therapy made me feel like I was bat-shit crazy.'

WEAK CENTRAL COHERENCE

There's an awful lot of theories that float around about autism. Some of them hold merit, some of them seem dubious, and others are downright bloody insulting. However, this next little bit of research published in 2010 did put a smile on my face. A research team had been exploring a particular type of processing in the brain referred to as 'weak central coherence'. Without getting too technical about it, they believe that a brain capable of 'strong central coherence' can integrate information in a kind of broad brushstrokes way (Booth and Happé 2010). For example, rather than saying 'At the pond today I saw ducks, seagulls, pigeons, swans, sparrows and a heron', someone with a strong central coherence would probably say 'I saw birds at the pond today'.

However, **our** brains have a preference for details over gist (local over global) which despite being a significant advantage in thinking outside the box (spotting errors, noticing small changes imperceptible to others, remembering huge swathes of information) it can also mean that life is often really difficult to navigate (put simply, we can't see the wood for the trees, or better still leaves!!).

And it's not just the visual stuff either, imagine trying to decipher which are the important bits in a conversation using this kind of hardware. When someone asks me the (supposedly) innocuous question 'How are you?', I tend to feel like a deer caught in headlights. What is it that they want to know? How far back do I go? To what degree of detail? In those moments it's like my brain seizes up, there's just too many variables to calculate and yet what's the first question most therapists insist on asking? How are you doing today?

By the way I only recently learned that the **correct** response to being asked this question is actually 'Fine thanks, how are you?' (Nobody **actually** giving a rat's arse how anybody is. Go figure.) It's not so much that we don't understand **what** is being said it's just that there's too much information coming in and our brains struggle to filter out what the key parts are (seeing all the ingredients at once rather than 'the cake').

The research team devised a basic sentence completion task in which participants were asked to provide an answer (a little bit like Family Fortunes). Have a go yourself and don't overthink your first response!

1. You can go hunting with a knife and...
2. In the sea there are fish and...

If you're like me, you may have answered:

1. You can go hunting with a knife and... fork
2. In the sea there are fish and... chips

Apparently (and take this all with a pinch of salt on your fish and chips) my knee-jerk reactions would indicate that my brain favours local over the global. Perhaps this is why so many of us have a distinct sense of humour, a sharp wit and love of word play. However, if you said:

1. You can go hunting with a knife and... gun/bow and arrow
2. In the sea there are fish and... sharks/whales/lots of sea life

your test results would indicate a strong central coherence though I'm not sure this would be a generally reliable way of testing for autism!

A DIFFERENT PLANET (I FEEL LIKE AN ALIEN!)

The other big problem we encounter is that we don't always understand the implicit or explicit rules and systems of the dominant (neuronormative) social order. Or we do but perceive it as fundamentally flawed, pointless and inefficient. All cultures have a particular set of customs, beliefs, values and behaviours which they believe are correct and determine how people should act. This social engineering aims to help us flow together. We all know where we stand and what to expect. Whilst the rules and standards are largely there to protect us, let's remember a few examples (regrettably not all from the past) which many people blindly followed:

- patriarchal hierarchies
- racial segregation
- slavery
- children being taken off unmarried mothers
- locking people in asylums for reasons such as laziness, overthinking, PMS, masturbation and novel reading
- corporal punishment
- female genital mutilation
- human sacrifice
- burning LGBTIQA+ people and witches (sensitive folk who were most probably very definitely neurodivergent) at the stake.

The point is that just because something is considered to be **the way things are done** does not mean it is right. Yet how many of us have gone through a lifetime of bullying, shaming, humiliation and ridicule for banging our drum to a different beat? How many of us have masked so hard that by the time we discover we're autistic later in life, we haven't got the foggiest idea what we really like, let alone who we actually are.

In psychotherapy the task of most people is surprisingly similar when you get down to brass tacks. Somewhere along the way the authentic self has become compromised and the person's mind and body alerts them of this by sending out distress signals of anxiety, stress or depression. In humanistic approaches (e.g. Gestalt therapy, person-centred therapy, existential therapy) we invite our clients to move towards that which feels right for them so that they start to feel aligned with who they truly are, and not who they have been conditioned to be by family, friends and society at large.

The extra complication we face as autistic clients is that we've been told our feelings, needs, preferences, wishes, desires, intensity of our passions, and even our thinking, are **wrong**. If we were discussing an abusive relationship here we would use the term 'gaslighting'.

It breaks my heart to think about how our natural-born instrumentation for recognizing patterns, sensing the unexplainable, carrying out deep and complex analysis and observing precise details is so accurate, yet around 80% of my clients claim to not know what they should be doing. Only by learning to trust our own feelings and observations can we begin to make choices that are right for us and create neurodivergent-friendly lives that better suit us.

'But, Steph, how on earth can I do that when I'm not sure what my **feelings** are?' And that's a very good point for my clients to raise because many of us will struggle to identify the inner sensations of the body which may provide clues. But why do you assume your feelings need to provide the clues? Isn't that the whole point, that we have a different way of experiencing the world and therefore need to tap into our own personal intuition?

- You may be more cognitive and enjoy figuring out a way forward through a detailed pros/cons assessment method.
- You may notice signs and coincidences and feel you are being guided along a particular path.
- You may feel tired by one set of circumstances and energized by another.
- You may (like me) have an imaginary friend (David Bowie) who talks to you and tells you what to do. And yes I know he's not real.[1]
- Or you may have a trustworthy connection in your life

---

1   Or do I? [twiddles moustache]

who can help you bring your truth to the surface when it feels buried under a million miles of spaghetti.

• You may enjoy journaling, meditation, dream-work, or seek spiritual direction through things such as tarot cards or attending faith groups.

Expecting us all to lean into feelings to provide answers is to interpret the autistic experience through a neurotypical standard.

DELAYED PROCESSING

Another challenge we may face is that due to our neurological differences we tend to have a slower communication processing speed (Haigh et al. 2018). This can be bloody frustrating (and sometimes embarrassing) when the world requires us to think on our feet and engage in the type of rapid-fire-surface-conversational-ping-pong favoured by neurotypical folk.

We have to take an in-the-moment conscious inventory of what is actually being said (listening, interpreting non-verbal communication, understanding, filtering out the key point from a bunch of endless possibilities) and **then** thinking of how best to respond, and **then** actually responding whilst monitoring your own delivery (a three-part system if you will). But not only that, we also have to do this with impaired neural pathways in the sensory, prefrontal, hippocampal, cerebellar, striatal and midbrain regions (Kumar et al. 2019). It's hardly surprising that so many of us insist on watching Netflix with the subtitles on...

However, it is important to note that in many areas (like visually) we can actually process information much quicker than most people (our brains running in a kind of high-level Matrix-esque code and forming less obvious connections); and we often have above-average IQ, and enhanced working memory (Remington, Swettenham and Lavie 2012). It makes perfect sense then that our delayed processing can also affect our feelings with one of my clients describing how they seem to have an 'emotional incubation period' before they can fully understand something that's happened.

I frequently encounter individuals who cannot understand why they are in autistic burnout, yet when we start to unpack their timeline there's usually a very clear cause and effect going on. But it's as if our past emotions just linger around in the body and psyche being unprocessed and building up like a plaque over time.

'Delayed emotional processing might be the reason people look at me like I'm an unfeeling robot with no empathy which couldn't be further from the truth. My girlfriend told me some upsetting news a few weeks back and because I didn't respond appropriately (as she wanted me to) we ended up having a row and I felt ashamed I couldn't be more supportive. I just needed time to think everything through, to understand what it all meant, and how I could help. I can't think that quickly but it doesn't mean I'm not sensitive or don't care.'

'I think my therapist gets angry with me because I tend to do all my thinking outside of sessions, when they've made it clear I am to think about things with them. But I need quiet alone time to properly think, in a social interaction I don't really know how I feel – I'm too caught up in concentrating, feeling anxious and performing – there's too much noise going on. I hate how they won't take me at face value. I need time to process.'

It's vital we start to consider the implication of this in therapy rather than just expecting clients to know how they're feeling in real time. Meltdowns rarely (if ever) come out of the blue and our #1 task is to get savvy and figure out how we can best avoid or mitigate them in the future. Will we ever get this system perfect? Of course not, I had one yesterday and I expect my neighbour assumes they're living next door to Begbie out of 'Trainspotting'. But at least one good thing can come of it – my body is telling me that I am at full capacity and that I need to go back to the constantly shifting energy accounting drawing board if I am to focus on feeling better.

A DIFFERENT PERCEPTION OF THE WORLD

It's quite a trippy philosophical concept to wrap your head around on first inspection. One would assume that if a group of people were stood around a table looking at a red apple in the middle that we would all be having pretty much the same experience. However, the truth is that each individual will be having a completely different perception based on a variety of influences, such as:

- our sensory capacity
- personal associations
- cognitive biases
- energy and stress levels
- feelings
- countless other factors.

Synaesthesia

Until recently I didn't realize I had synaesthesia, which affects 18.9% of autistic folk (Baron-Cohen et al. 2013) and is thought to be three times higher than in the general population. In simple terms synaesthesia is where sensory cognitive pathways merge in the brain and those of us with this as part of our profile may be able to see sounds, numbers might be perceived as a particular colour, words might trigger a taste or feeling (curiously my two favourite words are 'frustrating' and 'difficult' – both of which sound twinkly and magical to me despite their meaning!), or any other kind of unique blending.

One of the things I typically experience is that sounds are felt in my body as a visceral ripple – a bit like when you see the cup of water vibrate in 'Jurassic Park' when the T-Rex is having its jolly day out. Another thing I get is that touch (particularly unexpected micro touches like a fly illegally parking on your leg) can feel like I'm being tasered. Zig-zag lightning bolt patterns, geometric or tessellating shapes flash across my eyes and I hear a noisy electrical buzzing noise in my head. I just assumed this was how everyone experienced life.

Even without synaesthesia, given our unique neurological wiring it shouldn't come as a surprise that our own interoception (the internal feelings from inside our bodies, for example heart-rate, respiration, autonomic nervous system activity, emotion, thirst, hunger) and exteroception (e.g. sound, sight, taste, temperature, touch, where we are situated in space etc.) are also different. Meaning that it might not be easy (or even possible!) to translate our experience to a neurotypical therapist.

I feel a bit concerned that many mindfulness-based approaches for autistic people tend to focus on building or improving interoceptive awareness skills thought to help us with identifying our emotions. I can't help feeling they have limitations.

This morning I feel absolutely rubbish, I'm clearly unwell and massively struggling with a virus of some sort. But if you were to ask me what the symptoms are I would tell you that I feel like my blood has turned to bleach, there are a million electrical spiders rushing around my head, my face is made of a transparent gel-filled cube and it's as though I'm levitating above space and time. If I were to ring up my local GP and explain this to them they would think I've gone stark raving bonkers or been on the edibles.

Alexithymia

You may also be familiar with the term 'alexithymia' (the word originating from the Greek meaning 'without words for emotion'). It incorporates a range of difficulties in describing and identifying feelings (internal and external) affecting a whopping 50% of those of us on the spectrum (Kinnaird, Stewart and Tchanturia 2019). Not being able to accurately read our own states is highly likely to mean not being able to read the states, clues and intentions of others, no doubt accounting for some of the social errors and character misjudgements we face.

Later on in the book we will consider what this means for approaches such as cognitive behavioural therapies, because how can they claim to be successful if we aren't aware of our internal states?

The Valence Arousal model (not as sexy as it sounds)

Something that I have found really helpful in my own work (and life!) is the Valence Arousal model which was developed by James Russell and Lisa Feldman Barrett (see e.g. Kuppens et al. 2013). Rather than the 'feelings wheel' (which is where therapists ask clients to colour in an emotion they are having, which can be difficult to pinpoint) the Valence Arousal model helps us to think about emotions in terms of just two factors:

- pleasure/displeasure (valence)
- intensity (arousal).

If you can imagine two intersecting lines so that you basically have a cross, at the top of the vertical line (north) you would have high arousal and at the bottom (south) you'd have low arousal. Then on the horizontal line, on the left (the west position) you would have displeasure and on the right (east) you'd have pleasure. Using this system right now I would be able to identify that I'm feeling fairly under-stimulated (low arousal) with a smattering of displeasure – feelings in this south-westerly position (I sound like I'm reading the weather now...) would include emotions such as tired, bored and depressed, which is absolutely right – I'm knackered!

'My therapist says I have trouble identifying and communicating emotions, but I don't think that's true. I just talk about my inner and outer sensations in an abstract way he doesn't understand. He's even given me an "emotions wheel", but it feels frustrating having to describe the indescribable to people who just don't get it. In certain cultures there are emotional words with no equivalent in the Western world. I really think therapists need to view autism as a culture and stop trying to convert us.'

'It pisses me off that the medical community talks about autistic people not being able to identify and label emotions "correctly" as if we're all idiots who can't distinguish a smile from a frown. It's not that I don't understand feelings, it's that my body is sending me white noise – I think anybody would be hard pushed to hear what signal was being broadcast over the interference. My therapist made me feel like I was getting therapy wrong because I couldn't describe my experience. I had no desire to go back or even try therapy again in the future.'

Professor Tony Attwood reminds us:

> It's not that autistic people are being difficult in sessions, it's just a difference and it's important to accommodate those differences. If you had a client from Madagascar for example, you wouldn't expect them to share the same culture as you do. Autism is no different.

When I find that neurotypical people are having difficulty understanding my perceptual experience compared to their own, I often use the example of having a fear of public speaking (also known as glossophobia), which is thought to affect around 77% of the general population. To that group, getting on a stage and delivering a speech to hundreds of people would feel like a terrifying ordeal. I think it's fair to say they'd rather be having small-talk-chit-chat over coffee with a bunch of strangers in the lobby. Yet for me the coffee break sounds like the **most** terrifying part (even just thinking about it is making me feel a bit dodgy to be honest).

THE DOUBLE EMPATHY PROBLEM (AND IT IS)

In the late 1950s a psychologist called Carl Rogers came up with a new approach to psychotherapy, which he would call 'person-centred therapy'. Without getting too technical Rogers (1957) believed that human beings have an innate capacity to transform and heal, and that under the right conditions (he came up with six) a psychologically distressed individual could learn to accept themselves and undergo a transformative positive personality change.

At the heart of this approach is **empathy** – the therapist must have an empathic understanding of the individual's inner world, and that empathy must also be received by the client. It's no good a therapist feeling empathy for a client if the client doesn't feel it back. Without this shared resonance the therapy is unlikely to work. But hang on a minute. What's this?! The double empathy problem?! What's that when it's at home?!

Well if you haven't heard of it before the double empathy problem (despite the idea kicking around since the 1990s) was first brought to mainstream attention by Dr Damien Milton, a British sociologist, social psychologist and major advocate of autistic rights (diagnosed himself at the age of 36) – who published a fantastic paper on it in 2012.

As we know, according to the 'Diagnostic and Statistical Manual of Mental Disorders', autism is a condition which affects social-emotional reciprocity, causes problems for us in being able to understand verbal and non-verbal communication and presents challenges when it comes to developing and maintaining relationships. The suggestion behind this is that there is only one acceptable way to communicate and we're (obviously) the ones who are getting it wrong.

In his work Dr. Milton explored how communication is not simply the job of one person but of both parties involved, and that a mismatch in understanding is responsible for any kind of breakdown. If I cannot understand my French cousin, should I arrogantly label **them** as lacking communication skills (tu es un crétin!). Or should I accept that I'm also responsible for establishing a mutual connection? Simply put, neurotypical people have as much trouble understanding **us** as we do **them** as also explored in a rather wonderful study entitled 'How easy is it to read the minds of people with autism spectrum disorder?' (short answer, not very!) (Sheppard et al. 2015).

In our discussions around the topic, Sarah Hendrickx (an amazing autistic author, diagnostician, trainer, olive grower, basket maker and eater of picnics) summarized this really well stating:

> It seems obvious that autistic people can often empathize beautifully with other autistic/neurodivergent/marginalized people, but can struggle with neurotypical people who have differing values and priorities, which can be more socially or emotionally based. It is also clear that neurotypical people have no clue what autistic people value and prioritize and hence the problem arises. Due to autistic people being in the minority, they are more likely to be considered wrong/cold/harsh etc. than simply different. In my experience, there is judgement from both sides about what matters and what doesn't emotionally and It seems tough for either party to see the other perspective.

Professor Tony Attwood echoes this sentiment:

> Communication is really a two-way street, but the average neurotypical person who cannot think, perceive or feel like an autistic person will have great trouble in correctly reading the situation, thereby causing discomfort and resentment for not responding in the 'conventional' way.

Empathy is an incredibly complicated area of study, and it's important to distinguish between the different types:

- emotional empathy
- cognitive empathy
- compassionate empathy.

Emotional empathy

Emotional empathy (also known as affective empathy) is when we can sense what another being is feeling (I'm including the animals in this too, not just people). I cannot watch an advert on television which features animal cruelty in any way, I will literally start crying hysterically because the idea of a beautiful creature being tortured is abhorrent to me. In fact, a former client of mine once described how she would always buy the battered old tins of soup in a supermarket nobody wanted because she felt sorry for them (I know exactly what she means).

The majority of clients I work with often describe having hyper-empathy (too much empathy), which can make life very painful to navigate. For them, they are like a sponge to other people's negative emotions and vibes. They can walk into a room feeling perfectly happy and then suddenly develop a deep melancholy. What is happening in that kind of situation is that the crowd has infected them in a kind of psychic contagion probably as a result of our heightened exteroception response.

Cognitive empathy

Cognitive empathy on the other hand is the way in which we figure out what another person is thinking or feeling. This may (or may not!) be difficult for us due to the differences in perception described in this chapter. Neurotypical people often talk their way vaguely around a subject avoiding the direct point as if that's rude. Instead we are expected to **infer** meaning, which can feel like a bloody minefield when there could be a thousand variables to choose from!

This is often the type of empathy we have most difficulty with, but I feel it's important to stress that we can work on this with a little practice. During my time at university we were required to do various exercises in learning to build empathy, and believe me when I say some of the trainee counsellors on our course were absolutely rubbish at empathizing! I try to put myself in the shoes of another person as if I were a character in a film – What might they be going through? How would they react? and so on. These days in my sessions it's as if I hear the client narrate their own story which I watch on a kind of TV screen in my mind and immerse myself into the plot.

I think back to my early life and realize I was probably not very good at this aspect of empathy at all. I was always saying the 'wrong thing' and being told off for responding in an 'impolite' way. I also can't help but wonder if that's why eye-contact can feel too much for those of us who are hyper-empathic, it's like we see too much in another person's eyes and can't cope with the intensity of feeling.

Compassionate empathy

Finally, compassionate empathy is about how we offer support to another person who might need our help. When neurodivergent individuals see someone who is upset we may want to offer our support by sharing a similar experience (trying to find mutual connection), being logical about the problem (trying to find a practical solution) and potentially avoiding physical touch such as hugs, hand-holding or arm-stroking (because we might not like it if someone did that to us). Heartbreakingly this can often be misconstrued as **not** caring – we are wrongfully accused of making it about us (egotistical), being bad listeners ('I don't want your advice I just want to vent!!') and cold ('What's **wrong** with you? **Normal** people would want to comfort someone who's upset!').

The idea that autistic people don't have empathy is very upsetting to me. Like everyone else on the planet, our ability to feel empathy will fall somewhere on a spectrum (there are plenty of neurotypical people who don't experience empathy either, but rather than berate them we tend to elect them instead.)

Going back to Dr. Milton's point about the double empathy problem, you can really start to see that whilst some of us may struggle to read the thoughts and feelings of others, most neurotypical people also struggle to read the thoughts and feelings of us! Why are we the ones expected to fit in with everyone else? Wouldn't it be better if when Aunt Patricia starts yelling at you, 'Uncle Roderick has just died and you haven't given me so much as a hug!' that we feel confident to assert ourselves and respond, 'Actually, I'm not the sort of person who enjoys hugging but that doesn't mean I don't care, and I'd be happy to help you sort out his things when you're ready.'

Assumptions are typically made in the absence of clear communication and maybe part of our journey is to educate others about our autistic ways rather than presume they'll just know. Sir Simon Baron-Cohen (cousin of Sacha/Ali G) declared that autism was an 'empathy disorder' (Baron-Cohen and Wheelwright 2004), which sadly paved the way for an unintended legacy of pain and misunderstanding.[2] Far be it from me to argue with Cambridge University's Autistic Research Centre Director (who am I kidding, here we go...), but as a neurodivergent person and someone with the incredible privilege of peering deep into the psyches of other autistic people (not just observing them in well-designed research studies), I simply cannot relate to his perspective.

I am yet to meet an autistic person who wasn't deeply concerned about hurting other people's feelings. In fact, as a group we are

---

2   You only need to do a Google search such as, 'autistic people don't have empathy' to instantly find 15,000,000 results.

recognized for our sense of fairness, morality and justice. If we didn't have empathy, then possessing those positive traits would make no logical sense (we'd all be sociopaths). Of course, empathy and the way we communicate it may certainly fall on a continuum, but isn't that the same for all humans?

Much of Baron-Cohen's work is built around his 'extreme male brain' theory of autism (that we experience the world through a male lens and prefer stereotypically male topics) (Baron-Cohen 2002). But this is commonly disputed within both the neurodivergent and research communities over claims of neurosexism and misinterpreting biological data. In a nutshell, Baron-Cohen hypothesizes that these sex differences exist on a scale where at one end there is 'female' (empathy brains) and at the other end 'male' (systemizing brains). I am saying no more on this topic other than the fact I am a highly sensitive, socially aware, nurturing and empathic female with a love of a tidy spice jar cupboard. Make of that what you will.

Baron-Cohen has made it quite clear through the media that his research is often taken out of context and that involving the autistic community in his work is very important to him. But repairing that broken trust and challenging entrenched public perceptions of autism seems a tricky undertaking. Stereotypes don't vanish overnight, particularly when clickbait headings aren't all that exciting.

If we are considered to have difficulties with 'theory of mind' (the ability to read or predict another person's internal state such as their thoughts and feelings), well, it works both ways, pal!

BOTTOM LINE

Our autistic brains are structured differently with more grey matter volume overall (Gennatas et al. 2017), have greater neuroplasticity (Desarkar et al. 2015) and, according to one 2017 study (Valnegri et al.), are thought to have around 50% extra synapses (shut the front door!). These idiosyncratic and unique configurations are the reason so many of us may be gifted in certain areas but struggle in others. And wherever we find ourselves on the spectrum let's remember, there's no such thing as a typical autistic brain any more than there is such a thing as an average (normal) neurotypical one.

Authors like Thomas Armstrong (2015) argue that neurodiversity is in fact an evolutionary advantage. I'm pleased to say that it does feel that others are slowly shifting to this way of thinking.

Autistic therapist James Barrott adds:

> I see neurodiversity as a different and equally valid way of operating. It isn't about how autistic people can adapt to be less autistic and to be able to pass as more neurotypical, it is more how can autistic people honour our process whilst also recognizing that we need to be able to gain support from the world as it is.

Given that we are literally having a different kind of perceptual experience (I even think of myself as a different breed of human to be honest), what are the implications of this in the therapy room? How important is it for therapists to be fully cognizant of these issues? Can they really help us if they aren't? Let's take a look in the following chapter.

SUMMARY

- Autistic people have an entirely different sensory perspective of the world compared to neurotypicals.
- Our brains automatically focus on the detail rather than the gist, making it hard to see the bigger picture. But this can be advantageous in many applications (fault finding, pattern recognition, etc.).
- Our neurological differences can make it difficult for us to understand dominant cultural norms and expectations often resulting in shaming and ridicule (leading to relational trauma).
- Perceptual differences such as alexithymia and synaesthesia may present challenges in therapies which ask us to describe our emotions.
- Issues relating to the theory of mind are actually a two-way concern (the double empathy problem). That autistic people don't have empathy is a myth.

Chapter 4

PROBLEMS WE MIGHT ENCOUNTER AND WHY TRADITIONAL THERAPIES MAY FALL SHORT

As therapists (here in the UK at least) it isn't our place to diagnose clients and there are no professional pre-requisites to understand anything about neurodiversity in order to practise. In my clinical experience the majority of undiagnosed or newly diagnosed clients typically arrive with incredibly high markers for depression, stress and anxiety. But when we start to peel back the layers, we often discover that the distress is actually secondary to unmanaged autism – that is, a result of trying to unsuccessfully contort ourselves into a neurotypical shaped person. I believe this raises a very worrying ethical dilemma – how many of us will be wrongly medicated or treated for something that isn't actually wrong with us in the first place?

If we explore some of the common reasons people tend to go to therapy (as we will in this chapter), we will soon notice that at times the off-the-shelf advice dispensed by clinicians may not actually work for us and may in fact make us much, much worse. In this section of the book I want to present an alternative perspective on some of the typical challenges we may be facing. We can then open up a dialogue with our therapists and make sure they're hearing us, and not just making assumptions based on their own way of viewing the world.

Of course, as we explored in previous chapters, our neurology and psychology do a complicated dance together, we are a neurodivergent brain going through stress and trauma and cannot separate the operating system from the event. But it is my hope that this chapter may help you to reframe your own situation and prompt you to ask yourself: Do I actually need therapy or will adjustments in my everyday life resolve the issue?

Each week I receive dozens of online messages on the socials from neurodivergent people describing how they have experienced harm at the hands of well-meaning therapists, creating new trauma where there was none before, or compounding old wounds. I have been deeply moved by your experiences of being failed, invalidated and misinterpreted, even though your words, senses, and intuitive experiences were completely correct and beautifully articulated.

One of the most frustrating things I see is that despite huge amounts of anecdotal evidence from the autistic community, unless things are substantiated by mainstream science it's as though they don't exist. Modern psychology lags far behind what we already **experientially know** to be true. The sad reality is that the bulk of financial resources spent on exploring autism are directed to programmes which provide early interventions, treatments, finding 'cures' and working towards stamping out this 'epidemic'. Let's be honest about who evidenced-based anything is really going to benefit – the corporations and pharmaceutical companies. There are most definitely other types of evidence in existence (e.g. population studies) but it seems that 'evidence-based' simply refers to randomized clinical trials (not necessarily carried out on any large scale either).

Carrying out research around autism is always going to be just that little bit harder, as from an ethical stance we are considered to be a vulnerable group. Yet it never fails to surprise me just how white, adolescent and male the participant samples usually are. Such 'official results' (which generally conclude with, 'more research around this area needs to be done' – but that gets largely glossed over) then become our news clickbait headings. These in turn become public misinformation and myths, reinforcing existing stereotypes. You can explore this narrow representation yourself: try pulling up five completely random studies on Google Scholar using the search term 'autism spectrum disorder'.

Where is the representation? Where are the women, non-binary, trans groups, bisexuals, people of colour? How does this research teach me anything about myself?

Of course this isn't reflective of all research and there are a great many notable neurodivergent (and neurotypical) individuals and teams doing their bit to raise awareness. But given the limitations of the structures we find ourselves in, in my view real progress is painfully slow.

As mentioned at the outset of this book, it would be impossible to write a book listing **all** the reasons people go to therapy (I'd be writing into old age!), but I've done my best to incorporate some of your key concerns with alternative perspectives here. I think the reasons most people choose to go to therapy is pretty much universal (difficult relationships, anxiety, depression, addiction, confidence, grief, etc.), if only clinicians were able to set aside their assumptions and recognize that our surface presentations may actually be indicative of hidden autism we might well be onto something.

LIMERENCE

Perhaps a relatively unknown one to start with but a topic I think is incredibly important and may in fact be a dead giveaway that we're on the spectrum. If you haven't heard of limerence before it is a term coined by American psychologist Dorothy Tennov in the late 1970s to describe the kind of agonizing crush that many of us feel as part of falling in love (Tennov 1979). Teenagers in particular often experience this as a kind of all-encompassing, unable to eat, sleep or think of anything else affliction. Far from a potential romance causing predominantly happy feelings, it can feel more like an emotional rollercoaster with many people sinking deep into a dark depression if their limerent object doesn't reciprocate. It's almost like having intrusive thoughts, a kind of love-based PTSD if you will, where the entire universe is centred around one thing only – making the other person want you.

Most traditional therapies view limerence as an attachment wound, suggesting evidence of past trauma or an underlying mental health issue. Although there is little written about autism and limerence, there is an awful lot to suggest that we may have people as special interests (particularly if you were a socialized female). One of my clients shared how her romantic hyper-fixation on a close friend was **the** most overwhelming high they could ever imagine. They stated: 'It is my version of a highly addictive drug that can leave me floating one minute and pretty much suicidal the next.'

But is it just hyper-fixation at work or something else? When we fall in love our brains flood us with norepinephrine, oxytocin, dopamine, sex hormones and other delicious brain candy, which gives us that biological incentive to pursue our potential mate, partner up and ultimately procreate (whether you choose to or not is a different story!). Interestingly there are a number of studies which suggest that autistic individuals may have signalling differences when it comes to dopamine responses, the feel-good/reward hormone (Paväl 2017), as well as deficiencies in oxytocin, the love hormone (Rutigliano 2016).

I expect that to brains lacking in these hormones, a small rush would feel utterly intoxicating, like drinking a nice cold glass of water when you've been thirsty all day. We may spend a great deal of time thinking about our love interest, unable to switch off our thoughts and redirect them onto something else. We may even find ourselves retreating into a fantasy world which feels far better than the anxious reality we are faced with on a daily basis. We may convince ourselves that they are our perfect match and will surely make everything better in our lives.

Quick fix of a love high

A new love interest can trigger our hyper-focus and hyper-fixation (and may give us a boost of energy like a big mental stim!). But quite often the uncertainty of not knowing what will happen next can activate a kind of unclosed circuit in our brain, looping us into black-and-white thinking and dizzying ruminations. In the British television comedy 'Fresh Meat' (if you haven't seen it, you should, it's brilliant) one of the characters, Howard, who is autistic, describes his crush as a kind of Trojan Horse virus infiltrating his software which I think is really apt!

I hate having a crush on someone because it's simply exhausting and I could do without thinking about that person intrusively for the duration I am awake. We may **want** to get our work done, we may **want** to forget about the other person so we can concentrate, but it's like their mental image is made of sticky fly paper. This can lead us towards feelings of shame – seeing ourselves as needy, desperate or obsessive. We may bombard the other person with too many texts, over-call or over-share. I'm pretty good in this respect, although have an embarrassing history of drunk texting, which I once creatively resolved by purchasing a very reasonable mini timer lock safe off the internet... in your face, Flanders. (Since quitting alcohol I now use it to house emergency teabags.)

Modern dating shies away from blunt, direct and honest communication (especially at first) and to many of us the 'thrill of the chase' just seems like a pointless waste of time. Or as my neurodivergent friend describes it, 'psychological warfare.' Therapists may misinterpret our actions as self-sabotaging, deliberately pushing others away due to some deeper psychological reason. Yet if we map various aspects of the diagnostic criteria onto dating – engaging in repetitive behaviours (preoccupied thinking), having social communication issues, experiencing challenges with uncertainty and change, feeling very strong attachments and stimming (including visual stims – I work with many clients who describe how their partner's face provides them with a huge amount of comfort) – it can certainly look like limerence to the untrained eye.

Does that make me weird? (No!)

Simply the act of understanding what is happening can take some of the hypnotic sting out of it, making a person feel less weird and 'stalker-ish'. Some people waste years exploring attachment dynamics, trauma bonding and co-dependency issues, and figuring out why they choose emotionally unavailable partners, only to realize it was autism hiding in plain sight all along. I only wish I'd have known this as a young person growing up, I was always hugely embarrassed by how obsessed (even addicted) I was to the latest dark floppy-haired boy (and still am truth be told, although my current fixation is Pedro Pascal and I haven't got his number... yet). It would have been so reassuring to know that actually my neurology was just really excited and that it didn't mean I was a creepy weirdo.

> Intense interests are part of the autistic experience. These may be short-lived to lifelong, but the singular focus – usually one interest at a time – and the intensity – depth and all-encompassing nature – are the key. – therapist Sarah Hendrickx

SOCIAL ANXIETY DISORDER

For most people social anxiety disorder (also known as social phobia) is a highly treatable condition helped by approaches such as cognitive behavioural therapy, the goal of which is to help a person identify the 'irrational thoughts' considered to be at the heart of their fears. Whilst anyone can struggle with social anxiety at any point in their lives, often the root cause in an autistic person may not be to do with negative projections or paranoid beliefs, but may instead be due to the very real neurological differences which can cause us social difficulties.

To us the anxiety may arise out of:

- feeling confused during conversations (or in my case, not having a clue what is going on most of the time!)
- having to spend life ad-libbing
- not recognizing what is expected of us
- overstepping unspoken boundaries
- problems with reading and decoding subtext
- monitoring our own responses (did I give the right answer?!).

When I'm talking to someone it's as if I'm constantly observing myself – analysing how I'm coming across (am I using the right tone, words, body language, facial expressions?) in order to build that sense of free-flowing reciprocity neurotypical folk perform reflexively. Before diagnosis I tried everything to help with my 'social anxiety', including the well-known 'fake it till you make it' approach. I didn't realize that it was okay to not enjoy socializing much (introverted social preferences are generally considered unfavourable) and that my inherent neurological wiring made conversations tricky, draining and very stressful.

My exhausting compensations to pass for normal (masking) had fooled not only everyone around me, but also myself. Even now I have certain people in my life who don't seem to 'get' the mental hoops I jump through simply to participate.

As I sat down to write this book I thought about my late Nana, who was diagnosed with 'untreatable depression and agoraphobia' and medicated with Valium for 40 years. She rarely left the house and had no real friends to speak of, but I would cherish our conversations – I felt that she really understood me. We seemed to connect on a level that the other family members couldn't really understand and only now can I see she was probably autistic and struggling like hell.

'Years of confusing relationships, upsetting people and not knowing why, relational trauma, feeling different, exclusion (subtle or glaringly obvious), not sharing the same kinds of enthusiasms as others, speaking in depth rather than small talk, the list goes on, is bound to leave you feeling emotionally scarred. I went to cognitive behavioural therapy for a few months and the therapist just made me feel like I wasn't trying hard enough, even though I was doing the homework and putting myself out there. It didn't change the fact that a conversation feels overwhelming for me and that my brain has to work extra hard to keep up.'

'My therapist was amazing in helping me identify I was autistic. I had been referred to a mental health team for severe social anxiety but when we got into the work she realized that although I was struggling with worry about what others thought about me (thoughts like I'm weird and different) she was able to notice that I seemed really confused whenever I let my guard down (basically dropping the mask). I don't think I would have been able to stop masking had we not built up a close relationship, she was so gentle and never assuming. I always left sessions feeling on top of the world that someone, perhaps for the first time in my life, was actually interested in me, rather than filling in the blanks for themselves.'

Rejection sensitivity dysphoria

It is also worth noting that whilst not yet formally recognized as an official medical diagnosis – and usually talked about relating to attention deficit hyperactivity disorder – there is a lot of anecdotal evidence to suggest that autistic people can also struggle with rejection sensitivity dysphoria (RSD). RSD is where individuals experience a high degree of sensitivity and emotional dysregulation around the themes of being rejected, criticized, feeling like a failure or being embarrassed (either perceived or imagined), which many describe as an intense emotional or physical pain.

Unsurprisingly (because it doesn't 'exist'!) there are currently no studies to explore the links between autism and the condition. However, initial research believes that RSD is in fact a brain-based response and not attributable to trauma.

According to cognitive behavioural therapy, changing your thoughts about something will subsequently influence your feelings, yet in my work I've never seen an ADHD-er 'get rid' of RSD completely. In my professional opinion it's a bit like asking someone to see less of the colour green, or to stop burning as much in the midday sun.

If we consider how autism spectrum disorder involves differences in the processing of social stimuli – for example reading facial expressions, misunderstandings and miscommunication, or the amplification of neutral faces into angry ones due to our heightened interoceptive and exteroceptive responses (Black et al. 2017) – there's only so far we can go with **convincing** someone everything is fine if they just tried a bit **harder** and thought about things more positively.

Stuck in the mask

Sadly a common way many autistic people deal with the pain of social anxiety is by adopting a people-pleasing stance. They essentially ignore their true needs and wants in order to placate the other person and regulate their own internal states. One client of mine remarked how she didn't even know who she was any more, having spent so long trying to be the kind of person she thought everyone would approve of. She was desperate to unmask and start living a more authentic life but had received negative feedback from friends and family members when they had tried this. She broke down when she told me that her husband had commented, 'What's wrong with your face? Where's the old [name] gone? She used to be so much fun. You're so flat and boring now.'

'I wouldn't say that I have social anxiety as such but I have little to no social motivation. The problem isn't my preference, it's what society expects from me. The pressure to conform and push yourself to do things you aren't naturally inclined to do gives me anxiety. My last therapist essentially told me I needed to get a life, as if more social exposure would make me want to participate more. It only made me feel worse. I hate the way if I'm feeling burned out everyone tells you not to isolate and withdraw, but that's what makes me feel better. More social exposure just causes me more stress and burnout, I hate people enforcing values on me which harm me.'

Drink, drugs and addiction

It perhaps then comes as no big shock that many of us turn to other coping strategies, such as alcohol or drugs, to ease the pressure felt in social situations. I've had clients describe how having a few drinks before they go out makes them feel 'normal' as if their autism has temporarily faded into the background. I know of many friends who have wrestled with substance addiction in order to find some sense of escape from their emotional and sensory pain. Although generally unexplored there is some initial data to suggest that there could be a genetic link between autism and addiction, with a 2017 Swedish study (Butwicka et al.) finding that people with autism spectrum disorder (ASD) had a doubled risk of substance abuse issues, and was even higher in those with ASD and ADHD combined.

Unlike the other areas I'm looking at in this chapter (which I suppose you could boil down to 'Is the presenting issue the actual problem or is it autism underneath?') with dependency I would say we certainly need to honour both areas and seek appropriate professional interventions. We may naturally struggle with impulsivity, compulsions and repetitive behaviours and it is crucial we start to find ways of finding healthy coping strategies that will not harm us. I can't help but wonder if my mum could've been autistic too and that drinking was her way of coping. Sadly, I'll never know.

'Alcohol makes socializing much easier but the reality is most people only know and relate to a chemically altered variation of myself. That person isn't real and bears no resemblance to my actual character, which is quiet, solitary and shy. At one stage I got a reputation for being a party animal, but I didn't feel I could confidently live up to everyone's expectations without drinking. Everyone was so used to the mask and I felt trapped in a lifestyle that I knew was damaging my health and mental health. After I quit drinking I hardly saw anyone and now only have two real friends, where alcohol isn't needed to get by. They're both neurodivergent.'

ABUSE

Being autistic significantly raises our risk of finding ourselves in toxic, manipulative, controlling, coercive and exploitative interpersonal relationships. Sadly it's a well-known story. As I look back on my life before I was diagnosed, I can see how I was far too trusting, naïve, gullible and worried about hurting other people's feelings (even if they were causing me incredible distress). I assumed that everyone thought like I did and would therefore have the same principles, morals, intentions and emotional availability. When I observed negative or abusive qualities in others, I took this to be an indication of their inner pain and generally felt sorry for them.

Although my feelings were giving me some pretty big warning signs, my more powerful logic doubled down and went into problem-solving mode. How could I fix this person and make them better? It never dawned on me in my little Nemo fish brain that some people are just sharks. And not only that, but they enjoy being sharks too!

I was once in a long-term relationship with a seriously abusive man. It was like living with Jekyll and Hyde and I was never really sure what I was going to get next. But rather than validate my own pain, create boundaries and ultimately leave, it became my life's mission to 'solve' him (almost mathematically). I could rationally and logically understand **why** he was the way he was so it made sense to me that if only I spent enough time and energy on this conundrum we could work it out and live happily ever after. Errr... wrong!

I knew nothing about co-dependency at the time, or how autism means that we may struggle to work out the true (and sometimes dark) intentions of others. Despite him having so many red flags that he might have passed for a 1970s cheese and pineapple hedgehog table centrepiece, I felt like a total arsehole for abandoning someone who was clearly so messed up. All I could see were **his** ego defence mechanisms playing out, which left me dangerously out of touch with **my** own experience of suffering.

'I dated an abusive partner for years and it's really scary to think how obvious the abuse was which I explained away at the time. I was also in therapy at the time but I didn't know I was autistic. It sounds silly now but I just wanted him to like me – to feel like I belonged and fitted in somewhere. My therapist was really encouraging me to leave, but it felt like a betrayal to abandon someone (me obeying "moral rules") and would make me a bad person. I also misinterpreted a lot of the signals my body was giving me – in hindsight what I saw as butterflies and excitement (almost high) was my

> system being terrified and flooded with adrenaline. After he
> would upset me or hurt me he would always apologize and
> blame it on being ill, and it only made me more resolute to
> help him with these "psychotic out-of-character episodes".'

We make alluring targets for abusive types, we are often deeply empathic, kind, excellent listeners (because sometimes it's easier to listen than talk) and non-judgemental. My advice is to always trust your gut instinct and to stay away from anything which causes you discomfort, whether that takes the shape of a negative person, environment or situation. There is a big difference between avoiding situations because they might 'frighten us a bit' (and potentially limit our growth if we hold back) and actively protecting ourselves by not putting ourselves in harm's way.

Let me remind you, you are not responsible for fixing anyone in life, you are only responsible for keeping yourself safe. By all means support someone if they are on a journey and want to change (and you **want** to help them!) but don't get drawn into the orbit of energy vampires who only want you as a concerned audience member (think about it... if they **actually** changed and got better, how would they get their attention needs met?).

Self-esteem and emotional damage

Professor Tony Attwood shares how in his clinic, the issue his clients describe isn't so much about the state of being autistic itself, it's repairing the damage to our self-esteem caused by painful experiences at the hands of others. Research suggests that between 40 and 90% of us have been bullied at some point (Maïano et al. 2015), that 90% of autistic women have experienced sexual violence (Cazalis et al. 2022), perhaps relating to not fully understanding consent or being able to read danger signs, and that 50 to 89% of us have experienced interpersonal violence and victimization – emotional, physical, sexual abuses and financial exploitation (Pearson, Rose and Rees 2022).

As with all the themes explored in this section, there is rarely a clear cut answer as to why we may find ourselves in the kinds of situations mentioned above but I believe it's essential we dig deep with a skilled professional to uncover those reasons (neurological, psychological or both) so that we don't end up repeating the same experiences.

AUTISTIC BURNOUT AND FATIGUE-BASED COMPLAINTS

One of the regular problems my clients bring to sessions is the frustration that they cannot keep up with the demands of daily life with many (most) dealing with exhaustion and fatigue on an ongoing basis. I cannot take any credit for the following analogy which was described to me by a wonderful client of mine (let's call him T).

T thought about all future activities as holding a kind of gravitational mass which warps the fabric of flat space – the bigger the activity, the denser the mass and the greater the warping effect. He explained how having too many things on can feel like he's almost being sucked into the middle, whereas for many non-autistic individuals, such events can actually lift them – an anti-gravity if you will – 'I can't wait for the hen party at the weekend, it's going to be a-ma-zing!'

As he described this I was shocked by how this echoed the way I view life too, if my diary happens to be busy (and by busy I mean two appointments in one day) it's as if my brain cannot hold all the component parts and demands, and collapses in a state of overwhelm. It might not be easy or possible for us to put anything 'out of our minds', everything just building up and inducing anxiety caught in a kind of permanent waiting mode. I believe this is because everything we do is a **thought about** process. I don't just 'get in the shower' as if by magic, for me it's a huge undertaking – must get fresh towels, must switch heating on, must get clean clothes, must collect my toothbrush on charge... it's as if my brain is running the sort of programming code I used to see on my old ZX Spectrum (showing my age now), all of which is hugely taxing to consciously remember.

Why worry? Just chill!

It's hard to explain this to the average neurotypical person who may ask us what we're worrying about ('Brenda's wedding is three months away, so what?!'), but since everything we do comes with an energy cost (thinking/action) typically layered over executive dysfunction, the concern is that we may not have the necessary emotional reserves to pay for the future experience. Whether I have a deadline next week or next year is totally irrelevant to me, it's that I have an anxiety-provoking deadline looming over me until it is complete. It's as if the neural circuits in my brain cannot close until it is done, at which point it is 'done'.

Many of the mainstream self-help strategies encourage us to imagine 'turning anxiety into excitement', which sounds deeply minimizing to my mind. It isn't about us being negative overthinkers who just need an attitude adjustment, it's that everyday life hurts us in a way others cannot fully comprehend. Self-compassion and recognizing our limits are the things we really need to work on in therapy, not trying to figure out how to extract a pint of water out of a thimble.

Quite honestly the only time I am able to sit in physical tranquillity (and it's never 100% peace, there is always something niggling at my noggin...) is when I am totally alone in a room with zero stimulation.

We have less petrol in the engine

We start the day with fewer reserves than most people and because much of what we do is carried out at a conscious concentration level, akin to sitting an exam or being in a job interview, it's as if our internal warning systems are carrying out a primal assessment of predicted expenditure behind the scenes – can I actually carry this demand and for how long?

Whilst it would be unreasonable and rigid for us to simply dig in our heels and say no to everything (which would probably only leave us bored and lonely anyway!) we do need to start getting better at only taking on what **feels** right for us, using our in-born 'no thankyous' to ensure there is enough of us to go around. Being expected to contort ourselves out of shape to keep up with a neuronormative culture isn't going to work out well for us and will eventually culminate in serious mental and physical health issues – fatigue, burnout, anxiety, depression, high blood pressure, heart disease, diabetes, strokes, chronic inflammation and various stress-related illness. It really is very serious and not to be ignored.

Yes, but how can I stop being autistic?

I meet with a huge number of clients who come to me essentially asking how they can 'hack their autism' and compete with everyone else, as if they are in denial of their differences and carry internalized ableism.

What does a neurodivergent-friendly life look like for you? Why do you think you have to live in a certain way just because others do if it doesn't feel rewarding? When it comes to burnout, prevention is always better than cure, so rather than recover from one and dive straight back into how things were before (perpetuating a boom-and-bust cycle) might it be more helpful to go back to the drawing board and mix things up a bit? For me, it involved leaving a full-time well-paid career and taking a massive pay cut. However, that trade off means I get to spend time alone, be in nature, unmask as much as humanly possible, reduce demands and social expectations, and focus on my special interests.

I meet so many people riddled with guilt, believing that they do not measure up on a yard stick that didn't take our neurological differences into account. You wouldn't ask someone with dyslexia to read 'War and Peace' every day, or someone with dyscalculia to spend their lives doing simultaneous equations – yet we are expected to do things which we find hard and pretend it's easy peasy.

Back to basics, what do you want your life to look like?

I advise my clients to quite literally go back to basics and sketch out a sustainable world which works for them (any excuse for coloured pens and stickers!) taking into consideration the often harsh realities of responsibility and socio-economic factors. What **can** you change? What will make life easier for you?

The number 1 in ASD1 (see Introduction) means 'needs support'. It does not mean 'emulate a neurotypical existence, pretend it's manageable and feel like a failure when you can't keep up'! Some ex-colleagues of mine would always ask me what I'd done at the weekend, to which I would always answer... nothing! My energy levels don't magically recover after a good night's sleep but I always got the impression they thought I was lazy, weak, ineffective, avoidant or making excuses.

Burn, baby, burn

Dora Raymaker has done some fantastic work around defining what autistic burnout is and how it differs from the kind of generalized burnout experienced by a neurotypical person. She explains how we may face not only a debilitating mental and physical chronic exhaustion but also a loss of skills and a reduced tolerance to stimulus (Raymaker et al. 2020).

I think of autistic burnout as the dangerous tipping point on the scales where the demands placed upon us exceed our natural ever-fluctuating capacity. Sensory bombardment (piercing car alarms, dogs barking, florescent lighting, pungent smells) and social expectations (feeling pressure to engage in low-level social interactions all day long) will gradually deplete our batteries. If we do not actively replenish them, it will eventually drive us to the limits of our 'allostatic load' (Langelaan 2007) causing a total psychological and physical collapse.

Before I found out I was autistic I truly believed I was suffering from early-onset dementia or perhaps even multiple sclerosis. Three separate GPs diagnosed me with chronic fatigue syndrome, and I thought I was destined to never get any better. At the time of writing this, autistic burnout is not recognized as a medical condition and few general practitioners understand much about it. Their collective advice is usually to engage more with the world, cultivate connections, reduce social isolation, exercise more and change our attitudes! Great! More stuff to do!

Self-harm, suicide or suicidal ideation

You may be asking yourself what on earth suicide has got to do with autistic burnout, or even with the theme of the chapter (why traditional therapies fall short). Well, the sad fact is that since few clinicians are even aware of what autistic burnout is in the first place, not receiving adequate help for it can cause our lives to spiral dangerously out of control.

Our exhaustion may be perceived as laziness or an unwillingness to engage with therapy and broader social networks. I recall in my own experience that attending a therapy session once a week felt incredibly overwhelming – the social demand and expectation to perform at a cognitive level much higher than I was capable of in the midst of burnout only worsened my autistic traits and messed with my overall mental health. I often felt worse, not better for turning up to a session.

The feeling of severe autistic burnout is quite possibly the worst feeling I've ever had. Worse than the meningitis I had as a child which almost killed me, worse than the two hours of reconstructive surgery I had after nearly losing my hand, worse than being run over by a car, worse than my complex PTSD flashbacks, and worse than the worse hangover or flu I've ever had.

It feels like severe anxiety and severe depression rolled into one, mixed with a side order of immobilizing chronic fatigue, increased sensory sensitivities and a brain that simply won't work. I often describe it as feeling wired and tired – that is, a brain which is racing at a million miles an hour but won't power down to rest. In such a place I am in a state of complete overwhelm – my executive dysfunction literally preventing me from being able to think clearly and therefore attend to even basic self-care tasks. Brushing my teeth twice a day when burnout strikes is a major win.

But unfortunately many of us do not get the rest and respite we need from daily life to recover from this brain fire. We become more and more agitated as the frustration increases and often experience phantom physical ailments (my stomach will knot so tightly that it feels as if my colon is about to burst, my muscles ache, my joints are inflamed, and don't get me started on how bright light slices through my corneas).

Living like this is like feeling imprisoned in your own body. We may be desperate for release and an end to the suffering (suicide ideation), or we may feel so angry at our inability to perform the simplest things that we find ourselves bashing our heads, biting our wrists or clawing at our skin (self-injurious behaviour). I know because I do all of this when things get really bad.

I don't think autistic burnout is worse for any one particular group, however for those of us who are regarded as 'high-functioning' (again, not my words, 'high-masking' is preferable) the expectation to remain energy-consistent and perform at a particular level is often overlooked. Just because I had energy and could think clearly enough to write a book last week doesn't mean I can today under the thunderous cloud of burnout.

Many of the clients I work with have frequently been driven to the point of suicide and describe actual attempts on their own lives because they felt unable to cope. This crisis point is generally when we are admitted into hospital for 'psychological breakdown', even though the whole thing could be bloody avoided if we were given the tools, help, care and understanding to lead optimal lives in the first place.

There is a clear distinction between pathological self-harm and the kinds of self-injurious behaviours we see in autism (which is often a self-regulation/maladaptive coping strategy for alleviating inner pressure). Unfortunately not enough clinicians are informed enough to appreciate the differences and may misinterpret a momentary act of frustration as an indication of a deeper psychological disturbance. Had you seen me yesterday morning screaming at my laptop and crying on the kitchen floor because I'd lost the ability to read (temporary autistic skills regression), you might assume there was an underlying reason which needed wheedling out in therapy, when the reality is far simpler – it's just too much at this particular moment in time. To my mind professionals misunderstanding this distinction in traditional diagnostic or therapeutic approaches only adds to the mounting pressure we are already under. Feeling shamed, judged or misunderstood is not what we need in times of crisis.

That said, the links between autism and suicide or suicidal ideation are well-established with a worrying 66% of autistic adults having considered suicide and around half of that number making an actual attempt (South, Costa and Morris 2021).

Recently Dr Sarah Cassidy (University of Nottingham) and Professor Sir Simon Baron-Cohen (Autism Research Centre at the University of Cambridge) set about exploring the coroners' inquest records of people who had died from suicide to see if they had elevated autistic traits. They found that 10% of those individuals likely had undiagnosed autism (Cassidy et al. 2022).

Untreated and unsupported autism-related fatigue conditions destroy a person's quality of life. Self-help advice to take a warm bath, go for a walk or drink a glass of water are going to do very little if the underlying issue is that the person just can't cope with the life they already have.

What needs to happen?

It is my firm belief that every GP and therapist in the country should familiarize themselves with autistic burnout and consider this as routine screening protocol for patients who repeatedly return with fatigue-based symptoms without any underlying medical cause. The benefits of creating such a small pathway change could prove hugely significant for the healthcare services, for example less doctor's time spent on exploratory appointments, less demand on mental health services (since cognitive behaviour therapy may not be the best option for our needs), and fewer prescriptions of antidepressants being administered.

If you are interested in learning more about burnout, Amelia and Emily Nagoski (2019) wrote a book called 'Burnout: Solve Your Stress Cycle' (I don't think Emily knew she was autistic when she wrote it either!). And I can highly recommend the autistic burnout guide and worksheets produced by neurodivergent therapist Dr. Megan Neff.[1]

ANXIETY AND DEPRESSION

When our millions of blood test results come back all-clear, our baffling symptoms are typically regarded as psychological in origin and we may be offered antidepressants whilst we wait for our allocated free six sessions of cognitive behavioural therapy. It is important to note that here in the UK the National Institute for Health and Care Excellence (NICE) has a specific 'Do Not Use' recommendation marker regarding offering antidepressants to manage core symptoms of autism in adults (NICE 2021), and I worry that scores of us are on the receiving end of medical harm in this often lengthy limbo.

During my psychology training I was taught that there was always a fundamental reason behind anxiety or depression. Pretty much everything seemed to boil down to unprocessed trauma or a crappy childhood. I was once out for lunch with a good friend (a

---

1   Available to buy at https://neurodivergentinsights.com/neurodivergentstore

self-diagnosed neurodivergent) who shared how they 'had' generalized anxiety disorder. In my rookie arrogance I remember thinking to myself, 'Yes, but there's always a reason, you just haven't done "the work" yet.' Ten years later and having personally done all the work (heigh-ho, heigh-ho, heigh-ho, heigh-ho...), I can conclude that no, there isn't always a reason and that some of us are just built a little more sensitive than others.

We may certainly face a great number of additional challenges, for example loneliness, social alienation, negative or abusive relationships, poor life satisfaction, employment concerns, injustice... But there is a growing body of evidence which suggests that our mental health struggles may simply be rooted in neurobiological components, such as:

- a greater degree of arousal, executive dysfunction or emotional regulation issues (McVey 2019)
- a disproportionate risk of developing mental health comorbidities with a pooled estimation of lifetime prevalence of 27% and 42% for any anxiety disorder, and 23% and 37% for depressive disorder (Hollocks et al. 2019)
- 71% of young people with autism found to meet the criteria for at least one mental health disorder, with 41% having additional comorbidities (Simonoff et al. 2008)
- four times greater likelihood than neurotypical individuals to experience depression over the course of our lives (Hudson, Hall and Harkness 2019).

Atypical symptoms of typical problems

Professor Tony Attwood describes how the most common complaint in his clients is anxiety. He notes that if we could simply dissolve it away the quality of our lives would be phenomenally different. The added layer of complexity around this is that our anxiety may not present itself as typical symptoms (nervousness, a sense of doom, dry mouth, fast heartbeat, tightness in chest) but by a surge in movement and thinking. When I'm nervous, my body doesn't actually **feel** nervous at all (steady as a rock, Captain!), but my brain will go into overdrive with repetitive thoughts.

Our particular version of anxiety may include:

- a desire for greater routine and structure (which may look like obsessive compulsive disorder)
- a hyper-focus 'on steroids' (which may look like the kind of mania seen in bipolar disorder)
- greater difficulty tolerating sensory stimulation.

It is also worth noting that the majority of my clients who menstruate report that both their generalized anxiety and autistic symptoms get significantly worse as they enter the luteal phase (after ovulation around day 14) of their cycles. Premenstrual dysphoric disorder is another potential clue we may be waving under our GPs' noses indicating undiagnosed autism, with one study by Obaydi and Puri (2008) suggesting it affects 92% of us. Ninety. Two. Percent.

Similarly one of the things I often find with my clients is that despite feeling very depressed, they typically tend to score extremely low on standardized screening tests. We may not experience feelings of sadness, guilt, shame, poor self-worth or even negative thoughts, but instead have our depression make itself known through somatic distress, overwhelm, irritability, over-stimulation, unexplained fatigue or gastrointestinal issues. Personally I cannot even comprehend what stress 'feels like' on any psychological thought level. For me it tends to reveal itself through physical ailments, such as eczema all over my hands, dry wrinkly skin, stomach ache, arthritic pain, hair loss, insomnia and blurred vision.

Are autistic 'symptoms' just ways of coping with anxiety?

Typical strategies such as yoga or meditation may not necessarily work for us. Professor Tony Attwood explains how we have often spent so long supressing our emotions that to just sit with them can prove too overwhelming. Tony also makes a fascinating observation – if we look at the section B part in the autism diagnostic checklist of the 'Diagnostic and Statistical Manual', we can see that the 'symptoms' we are said to have might actually instead just be ways of dealing with anxiety. Examples are an insistence on routines and rituals (for greater predictability, less uncertainty), stimming (as a self-soothing behaviour), and having special interests (ways of distracting ourselves/thought blockers).

With a real push these days towards manualized therapeutic approaches, we must exercise caution if a one-size-fits-all-approach isn't working for someone. Tony adds that due to the incredible diversity in autistic people it's really about finding personal strategies which work. 'If a self-help book off-the-shelf works for you, great, but don't feel disheartened if it doesn't, you just haven't found your thing yet!'

IDENTITY CRISIS POST-DIAGNOSIS

Many of the clients I work with who were diagnosed in late adulthood describe overwhelming 'awakening epiphanies' when they realize that the life and personality traits they have found themselves with aren't entirely reflective of their true neurodivergent identities. I had an idea that post-diagnosis I would be skipping down the street, over the moon that I had 'found myself' after 40 years of exhaustive searching. Instead what I actually faced was an entire year of a mind-blowing existential crisis. It was as if my brain was going through a massive software update. I genuinely felt like I'd been hit by a bus – dizzy, confused, and enormously tired.

It's hard to imagine what this feels like unless you've gone through it and huge numbers of my clients share how they feel that they 'don't know themselves any more' and are 'questioning everything'.

Re-birth and re-evaluation of self

Taylor (1983) describes this kind of experience as a 'total re-evaluation of self and possible futures' in their work around cognitive adaptation. Whilst this may seem like a daunting task I personally view it as a gift and a rebirth opportunity. Our key struggle is often in

- giving ourselves permission to be exactly as we are
- rediscovering who we were before we were so conditioned to mask
- realizing that our feelings matter (begrudgingly going along with what others want is an instant route to mental health problems).

It will not serve you to continue in a role, dynamic or relationship that does not reflect who you are, and it may take some considerable work to go back to factory settings and realize you were issued the wrong instruction manual at birth.

One of my clients reported how everyone is used to her being funny, extroverted, quick-witted, and always available for everyone – when the truth was she didn't really enjoy socializing at all. She just thought she had to, and she pushed herself through weekly panic attacks in her desperate quest to fit in. I am reminded of Rachel Green in the TV series 'Friends' who after leaving her husband-to-be at the altar recognizes she is the master of her own ship. She muses on how all her life people have told her she is a shoe when she might in fact prefer to be a purse or a hat.

None of us were put here to suffer, and a crucial part of this post-diagnosis identity crisis is learning to establish firm boundaries and start listening to what really inspires us. This unmasking process involves creating a new self-narrative, re-examining our entire back-stories through a new and more accurate lens, and in my opinion a whole lotta grieving.

Grieving the loss of who we thought we were

In her 1969 book 'On Death and Dying' Elisabeth Kübler-Ross proposes that there are five stages of grief people move through when faced with significant loss: denial, anger, bargaining, depression and acceptance. In subsequent years there have been more stages added, but for simplicity of understanding let's stick with five. Before I moved into private practice I managed a bereavement counselling service and can clearly see the similarities in coming to terms with such a profound life-changing and paradigm-shifting experience and mourning the loss of someone we once held so dear. The familiar is gone and the path ahead looks unclear.

'Getting my diagnosis was just the first step and it took years for the dust to settle. In that time I changed my entire life realizing that I didn't actually want to work in finance (I subsequently opened an art and coffee shop) and leaving my otherwise wonderful marriage to my wife of 25 years and accepting I was queer. I had no idea a diagnosis would be so uprooting and loss-inducing.'

Steven D. Stagg and Hannah Belcher (2019) have carried out some interesting work in exploring a number of key themes from late-diagnosed autistic adults including the awareness of being different, support and coping, and the usefulness of a diagnosis. Many people describe a loss of hope, feeling that if they just tried a bit harder they would go on to be more successful, more confident and manage better. Accepting limitations can be deeply painful. One middle-aged lady client I worked with described how she felt it was time to give up on the fantasy self-actualized version of herself she thought she had to be. Rather than this feeling like an optimistic experience for her, it felt incredibly daunting and she described feeling lost without a map.

Try harder?! AAAAGH!

Positive thinking and daily affirmations can only take us so far. Sadly too many therapists buy into the idea that if we **really wanted** something, we could just achieve it with enough effort. Perhaps they don't realize that for many the neuronormative autistic experience is an effort too far.

It's often hard for us to say no to things, we are fearful of losing opportunities or other people's trust and regard for us, of looking incapable, of not being good enough. I am not for one moment suggesting we give up on our dreams (hell to the no!), it just might be that we need to recalculate an alternative route which hurts less. I have autistic friends who have taken three or four times the usual amount of time to complete an academic course. Not feeling able to sustain such focus and effort for long periods without it adversely affecting their health and wellbeing, but getting there in the end. But the big question we all need to be asking ourselves is: Where do we really want to go?

GENERAL

In my work I notice that the majority of clients tend to present with the same types of issues including:

- problems in their intimate relationships (not understanding why they aren't working or feeling bewildered by seemingly invisible expectations)
- struggles at work or in education (finding it extra hard to keep on top of demands that others seem to manage reasonably well)
- challenges in making or keeping friendships (such as wanting to have a social network but feeling overwhelmed by the amount of energy this will take to administer, not fitting in, or not being able to interpret others' intentions)
- feeling angry, frustrated or misunderstood by other people
- having a deep sense of shame and guilt but not really understanding why, just a sense that they are doing life 'wrong'.

The uneven autistic profile

I have had many individuals arrive at my office in floods of tears explaining how former therapists have made them feel as though they are stupid, lack common sense or are entitled princes and princesses not used to standing on their own two feet. One lady I worked with described how she could excel at running her own business but that her house was in complete disarray. It had gotten to the stage where she felt too embarrassed to invite friends over as rubbish piled up, washing-up covered every kitchen surface and dirty laundry seemed to breed when her back was turned.

Her last therapist had been less than sympathetic suggesting she just needed to buckle down telling her, 'Nobody **likes** doing chores, you just **have** to do them'. His punitive and condescending attitude reminded her of what it was like to grow up in a household where nobody understood her challenges either, further reinforcing her longstanding (false) belief that she was 'a bit useless'. Together we explored the impact of living with executive functioning impairments, which is believed to affect around 80% of us (Lai et al. 2017) causing issues with memory, planning, sequencing information and carrying out tasks (both initiation and execution).

She had spent her life 'winging it', trying to cope the best she could in the absence of specific coping tools or friendly support. Whilst much of our work together was around developing functionality and coping skills, she also had an ocean of rage to release as she reached her new conclusion: actually she wasn't useless, she was autistic and needed help. She decided to write a letter to her old therapist explaining that she had been diagnosed with ASD and that many of his assumptions about her had been incorrect and hugely damaging. She did not receive a response.

EATING DISORDERS

Whilst figures seem to vary depending on where you look, it is roughly estimated that around 30% of people with anorexia nervosa are also autistic (Babb et al. 2021). For me this particular topic is a highly complex and serious issue which has major therapeutic implications (life and death) if we are to consider some of the diagnostic confusion between the two conditions.

The overlap and interplay can be extremely confusing to untangle. It could be that somebody's disordered thinking and behaviours around food are manifestations of what is sometimes referred to as 'quiet autism' (particular in girls and women but definitely not always). I have met with dozens of clients in my own work who have been battling eating disorders, often for many years, before being correctly diagnosed as autistic. But it's important to note that a correct diagnosis of ASD doesn't mean an eating disorder will simply disappear in a puff of smoke. It is not like some mental health 'issues', such as anxiety, perceived as due to childhood trauma when actually due to sensory issues, which can be managed by careful matching of demands and environments. It is critical we understand both issues and treat them accordingly.

With eating disorders (which are mental health conditions) we generally tend to think about the main categories – anorexia nervosa, bulimia nervosa and binge-eating disorder (although there are more). However, symptoms may not always fit one neat box, and someone could be diagnosed with OSFED (other specified feeding or eating disorder).

Some of us may experience an obsession with counting calories, monitoring food intake and exercising. This may not necessarily be focused on weight loss as a goal (though could be), but as a way of managing difficult emotions, negotiating change and establishing safety rituals, routines and rules. Some of us may have a fairly limited variety of foods to choose from due to sensory issues with textures and flavours – perhaps diagnosed with avoidant/restrictive food intake disorder. Some may be pulled into orthorexia which is an obsession with 'clean eating'. Others may be locked into a binge/purge cycle.

Checking labels, following influencers, avoiding dining out, compulsively exercising (to offset calorie intake) can quickly take hold as a hyper-fixation special interest and may feel impossible to get out of (an example of restrictive and repetitive behaviours).

I have grown up around eating disorders, and some of my earliest memories are of my UK size 6 Nana patting her stomach and saying she was fat. After my mum's divorce she put on a great deal of weight and I would often hear her making herself sick after meals. She eventually dropped from a UK size 18 to a size 6 through starvation and would tease me for being chubby when I was a healthy weight.

One lady I spoke to described her medical trauma at not being supported by healthcare professionals. Despite being severely underweight she was told she couldn't be seen by their service because she was consuming too many calories at 900 a day (their cut off was 500). Pooky Knightsmith (autistic herself with a former eating disorder) is a big campaigner in this area and has a wealth of information on her website.[2] Treatments must be neurodivergent-friendly and make the necessary adjustments required for us to be able to participate (groups, regular attendance and insistence on particular foods may not be the best approach for us). These days if I encounter someone in a session who is struggling with disordered eating in any permutation I start to dig deep and listen carefully for ASD.

COGNITIVE DISTORTIONS (THINKING ERRORS)

In cognitive approaches to psychology we are taught that the root of our distress is our irrational thinking patterns referred to as 'cognitive distortions'. Their theory suggests that you can retrain your brain out of negativity by **recognizing** the thought, **challenging** it and actively **choosing** a different thought (replacement) instead. Researchers have come up with around ten major types of general cognitive distortions however the ones I'd really like to focus on are these pesky blighters:

---

2   www.pookyknightsmith.com

- black-and-white (all-or-nothing) thinking
- overgeneralization
- catastrophizing
- personalization
- mind reading/jumping to conclusions
- negative focus
- demands – living by fixed rules
- low frustration tolerance.

I would argue that these particular distortions are in fact classic examples of autistic thinking, dead giveaways in the therapy office, and not something we can condition ourselves out of easily (if at all!). Trying to convince our brains out of something which feels unbearable, replacing our safe routines and rituals with spontaneity, and putting positive spins on social situations (when we already feel terrified) seems like a recipe for disaster and may counter-productively lead to **more** stress, depression and anxiety (not less).

Social imagination does not mean what you think it means, Karen[3]

One of the things I struggle with is being able to imagine what the future will look like. In the past I have been accused by therapists of having 'a negative attitude' when in reality what I was dealing with was a lack of social imagination common to many of us. I remember hearing about autistic people having a 'lack of social imagination' and feeling seriously cheesed off. 'I'm creative actually, how dare anyone suggest otherwise! I write music, stories, make art – what on earth are they talking about?!' Only now I understand that a lack of social imagination has nothing to do with how creative you are, rather it's about our ability to predict the behaviour and intentions of others.

---

3 Apologies if you are actually just called Karen and definitely not a Karen.

Autistic thinking patterns distorting reality and optimism

I personally feel this is one of the reasons we tend to catastrophize. When we're caught up in a horrendous emotion (paired with an inflexible brain and challenges in self-regulation) it can feel like the entire world is ending. I frequently find myself crying face down on the bed (or kitchen floor) because something feels insurmountable.

I recently went through a breakup with a person I'd lived with for six years and whilst separations are universally hard, for autistics it can seem impossible to imagine a better life ahead. In my darkest moments I have caught myself in a blind panic that I will never find love again because I can't imagine **how** it will happen. This also ties in to the black-and-white thinking and overgeneralization patterns mentioned above (I am single now therefore I will always be single).

Similarly personalization (thinking that things apply to you when they don't) and mind reading (assuming you know what others are thinking, or imagining they think the same as you) are also common problems we face relating to theory of mind discussed earlier.

'My former therapist used to say I was being difficult and re-sistant, even accusing me of wanting to be miserable on one occasion. I used to think there was something wrong with me because I couldn't replace thoughts or reframe situations like he wanted me to, it just felt like I was lying to myself. It's as though there's no grey areas in my brain, something is either perfect or ruined, it's right or wrong. I can't help it but he made me feel like I was wasting his time.'

These days I try to accept that these quirks are simply part of who I am. I find that reading the Buddhist perspectives on suffering and acceptance has been a huge support on my own journey, enhancing my capacity to sit with the 'what-is'. I highly recommend the book 'Radical Acceptance' by Tara Brach (2003) if you would like to learn more.

OVERTHINKING, ANGER AND RUMINATION

Another example of autism waving in a therapist's face (wearing a multi-coloured sweater and a pair of deely boppers) are what I refer to as the frustrating Trinity of OAR (overthinking, anger and rumination). In the process of getting to the laptop this morning I have become angry about many things – a man coughing up and spitting noisily onto the pavement outside my window (gross, unhygienic), another man shouting loudly to a second person (at six o'clock in the morning – no respect or consideration), it being cold and getting out of bed feeling like a very difficult sensory transition, and the cat food pouch hurting my fingers with its fiddly tear-open strip (I simply detest opening boxes, envelopes, packages and such like as it always results in some kind of physical pain for me).

To a nervous system that feels like it's constantly switched on (fight mode to be precise) and living in a world full of unpredictability requiring constant threat assessment and conscious adaptation (using up our precious spoons), it's little wonder that the autistic experience is usually filled with emotions such as frustration, irritability, anger, dread, worry and a sense of wanting to be free from the pressure of never-ending demands.

We are told we 'overthink' – as if we have any level of control over it (errr, extra synapses, more connections, more activity!) – and encouraged to 'just relax.' From my observations in sessions I see that for most neurotypical people, externalizing angry feelings can help provide a gradual sense of relief. But I notice that, for many of us, talking about angry matters simply winds us up further (particularly something distressing over which we have no control like human rights violations, power abuses, animal cruelty, environmental issues, etc.) swirling us round in a kind of negative feedback vortex loop.

We may feel lost attempting to unglue ourselves, our well-meaning friends and family telling us to just 'do what feels right!' unaware that each of those possibilities is a separate universe for us which requires careful contemplation and analysis. I've even met autistic clients who have gone through a divorce wanting to know how long heartache will last and what practical sequence of steps they must take to outsmart the pain. We cannot mathematically process feelings. I'm sorry.

I am reminded of Sheldon Cooper from 'The Big Bang Theory' (who is thought to be autistic) who talks about how unresolved issues are uncomfortable for him, like an itch in his brain he can't scratch. As a child I was often told to forget about whatever was bothering me, and 'put it out of your mind'. I simply had no idea how to switch off in this way. I still don't, my problems piling up like dirty dishes and causing deep distress. Psychologists assert that rumination is essentially an unhealthy coping method for avoiding your feelings. But I believe when it comes to autism we may be better informed to start looking at the similarities and overlap of obsessive compulsive disorder spectrum neurology.

Rumination isn't optional for most autistic people

For me rumination isn't voluntary, it's more intrusive, as if I'm on the world's worst fairground ride. Many clients I work with have been incorrectly diagnosed with pure-OCD (where we have the distressing thoughts but not the compulsions). It tends to happen when there's a particular course of action I wish to take but my internal rules won't allow me (e.g. wanting to cut a toxic person out of your life but not feeling you're allowed to). Dr. Naomi Fisher simplifies this, explaining:

> Somewhere along the way what I learned was that my feelings were really bad and now I'm afraid of them. An approach like eye movement desensitization and reprocessing [more on this later] would be about really tapping into the feelings and separating them from the conditioning.

'I can tell when things aren't okay because my mind will not allow me to think of anything else. I will lose sleep, feel stuck and feel the most horrendous despair you can possibly imagine. It's like the tap won't switch off. I've gotten to the stage in therapy where I've described my situation so many times to so many different people that I feel like a stand-up comedian with a well-rehearsed piece. Going over something on repeat can imbue it with its own energy. By giving it so much attention, especially when it comes to autistic hyper-focus, you keep it alive – obsessional really. You can end up turning past trauma into a negative special interest.'

Rumination is like counting all the stars in the galaxy in an attempt to find a sense of system, place and structure in a wholly chaotic world. People are fundamentally messy, and even if we could study them on an atomic level we would still not understand **why** people do as they do. We are not privy to all their internal thoughts, experiences, histories, perceptions, values and cognitive distortions.

What we need to get better at is validating our own feelings **without** the 10,000 word essay on why you don't want to do something. Saying no to something (or someone) does not make you a bad person. It makes you a creator in your own life rather than being swept along with everyone's story. Therapists missing the obvious signs of autism mentioned here may in fact be doing more harm than good, foisting onto us an idea that if we just think about something enough we will solve our problems, rather than understanding that like pi we will just go on for ever without an additional clue or alternative perspective.

A little direction would be nice...

Therapists are taught that it isn't their job to give answers or advice, yet I strongly feel that's exactly what may be missing in sessions with autistic clients. The whole nature of being autistic is a constant state of analysing **everything** – your inner world, the outer world, dynamics, people, connections and thoughts. It seems that most neurotypicals enter into therapy in order to learn how to reflect, whereas for us it might be more about learning how to allow and accept.

Author and YouTuber Samantha Stein (Yo Samdy Sam) shares how for her therapy was low-key traumatizing:

> Whilst I don't think I've ever been to a terrible therapist, in my opinion treatment can feel like a series of micro-aggressions towards autistic people a lot of the time. Standard mental health advice doesn't always fit and exercises can seem a bit pointless. Before I was diagnosed I went to a private psychologist and she had all these techniques to help me 'release my anger' or 'visualize my feelings'. It left me

feeling really confused and wondering what on earth the point was. It's clear to me that the symptoms of trauma can seem indistinguishable from autism because society does not produce any untraumatized autistic adults.

Now that we've seen some examples of how the same presenting problem can essentially be two different sides of a coin (and therefore needing a different approach), how do we get to recognize the all-important danger signs, avoid therapeutic harm and crucially make sure that what we **say** isn't misunderstood by our therapists? This is the topic of the next chapter.

SUMMARY

- Some of the most common reasons people go to therapy have an alternative perspective on why the presenting issue could be autism hiding in plain sight.
- Off-the-shelf advice and psychological treatments may not work on autistics and in fact make things much worse.
- There is a danger that autistic masking and adaptation can result in serious mental and physical health consequences, including suicide ideation and attempts.
- Generalized 'cognitive thinking errors' may actually be indications of autism, given that many of the examples are typically neurodivergent ways of thinking.

Chapter 5

RED FLAGS AND RED HERRINGS

'I only had one thing to do this week, which by anyone else's standards doesn't seem to be that difficult at all.'

'What was it you had to do?' asked Veronica, with a furrowed brow you could keep pound coins in.

'I had to take a package back to the shop, for a return thing, you know, to Amazon, with the scanning machines, you know, the... things? I don't know what they're bloody called, scanning labelling posting machines?'

'Go on.'

'Well, things like that don't seem hard for other people but for me it felt like a total ordeal. First I had to **find** the package and make sure the bits were all inside, then I had to **leave the house** making sure I had all my bits and bobs with me like my keys, phone, purse... **then** I have to remind myself of what I'm going to say once I'm in the shop...'

'You have to **remind** yourself of what you are going to say? Why ever would you do that?'

I don't even understand the question. Doesn't everyone do that?

'Because if I don't, I'll forget and just stand there all blank and looking stupid. Then there was so much traffic, and noise, and people passing by – I felt like I was going to have a panic attack. And then once I got in the shop I couldn't find the thingamabob machine. Then my QR code wasn't working and I was getting really upset and nearly started crying. Then the woman came to help me and was asking all these questions and I hadn't prepared any of those answers...'

'Stephanie, I just can't understand the point you're trying to make. Nobody has to remember what they are going to say in an interaction, it just happens, naturally. It unfolds.'

Veronica's lack of empathy makes a big whoosh of anger bubble up inside me (which I force down as standard).

'And when I got home, I just couldn't do anything all afternoon, but I did what we talked about and reached out to a friend explaining how difficult it was.' (I thought she'd find that impressive, even just a little bit.)

'And what did they do?'

'Well, actually they turned it into a joke, as if I was being funny. She said, "Nothing is ever easy!" And to be honest it induced what I can only describe as a venomous psychotic rage which lasted for days.'

'She made a joke and you got angry?' (Oh my God, woman, stop stating the obvious! I just bloody said that!!).

'Yes, I went crazy, just screaming and jumping up and down, my heart felt like it was going to explode. And when I'm like that I can't bring myself down again. It's like my temper is too big for my body. One time I actually thought I was having a stroke, but it's weird because I'm not an angry person at all. More of a peace loving hippy really.'

'But **why** did you feel so angry?'

'Because I feel like that's all I've had my entire life from others. I'm explaining how difficult I find the simplest of tasks, how going into a shop and returning a package feels like I'm stood in the middle of a Japanese train station without a map, and everyone just laughs it off. It's not funny and the invalidation, flippancy and minimization makes me want to hurt myself. I can't cope and I don't fucking know why.'

I am desperate for Veronica to have the answers. This stuff stretches right back to when I was a happy little child, before Mum even drank, when I come to think of it. I remember her trying to get me to do my maths homework and I stabbed myself with a pencil in frustration. One time I actually tried to hang myself with a dressing gown cord because I couldn't complete Super Mario Bros. Why are my emotions so much bigger than other people's, and yet my face doesn't really give any clear indication of how I'm feeling inside? It's like my brain and expressions aren't fully wired together and I've been told I have a good poker face on more than one occasion (maybe a potential career move).

'It's clear that this is some kind of trauma, but unless you begin to explain where you think it comes from, we're unlikely going to be able to give it the space it needs to **breathe**.'

Why does this woman have to be so floral? She's like a pair of Laura Ashley curtains.

Later that evening my best friend comes over for our usual debrief. As I reach over to the bottle of wine in the middle of the table I manage to knock Collette's glass all over her. How can one human being be so clumsy?! I'm convinced I haven't caught up with the new dimensions of being a fully-grown adult human and still think I'm five years old. Apologizing on repeat I pour her a top-up doing silent counting in my head to make sure our glasses are both evenly distributed (anything else other than precision will bother me).

'Steph, I'm being dead serious now – I'm really not getting good vibes from your therapist. To be honest she sounds like she's on a bit of an ego trip or something. Every time you have a session with her you ring me up feeling worse, and I'm really starting to see a decline in your mental health.'

'Honestly, Coll, I agree with you but she gets amazing reviews online and I know things are often supposed to get worse before they get better. Perhaps it's just that I have a lot of ego-defences to work through?'

'And do **your** clients ever go through this kind of stuff?' she asks, her mouth going all small and tight.

'Not that I'm aware of. In our sessions it feels a bit like we're working on a collaborative project and generally they tell me how safe and supported they feel. I wouldn't dream of saying half the things Veronica says to me. She makes me feel like I'm a burden. But it's hard to figure out whether that's because she is making me feel like that, or whether I'm projecting onto her as she keeps saying. It's like my head is just going around in circles – my feelings telling me it doesn't seem right but my logic wondering if this is just good **deep** therapy. I don't like her really, I think she's a bit of a dick.'

'Mate, look, you've paid this woman a fortune and I've never seen you this bad in the entire 30 years I've known you. Hold that thought. I need a wee.'

As Coll scrabbles over the cushion fortress we appear to have constructed during our summit-level discussions I pull out my phone and flick through my therapy journaling entries. She's absolutely right, it doesn't seem to be going all that well, in fact the only times I feel like I've had a good week are the times where Veronica has just let me talk without disorientating interruptions (or she's been on holiday). I remember that she wanted to devote an entire session to discussing how I would feel when she is on her break, which I found utterly bizarre. I told her that I would be fine and would probably spend some time in the garden, but it was as though she just didn't believe me. Pregnant pauses filling the air with an acrid smoke she wanted me to do something with. Did she want me to say I'd miss her or something? That I needed her? That sessions are so important to me that I will surely go to pieces? Sod that, I'm happy to save the 70 quid and have a lie in.

Coll reappears and flumps herself back down. 'I don't know, man, it's obviously your call – I understand the whole darkest hour is before dawn thing you're getting at and you're worried about jeopardizing some kind of "cru-cial stage" [she makes little quotation marks with her fingers] but what if this is just bad therapy? How would you feel about writing it off as a mismatch, a learning experience and trusting your gut? Steph, I've known you since the first day of high school. You're not argumentative, you don't have problematic relationships with everyone... you don't suffer fools gladly, but that's a whole different ballpark! Veronica implying that you're re-enacting a difficult parental dynamic with her just gives her carte blanche to behave, in my opinion, grandiose and unprofessionally. How would you feel if I behaved in that kind of way?'

'It's such a weird feeling but I feel almost naughty as if I'm not **allowed** to terminate sessions, much in the same way I've ended up staying in toxic relationships. I think I have a rule that it's rude to walk away from someone and that you should be nice if you are to not hurt their feelings.'

'But they can hurt yours?'

'Yeah, that's not really working out for me is it? God, I hate conflict, I feel nervous about even broaching the subject with her.'

Coll's taxi pips its horn outside and in typical ADHD style she sets about a last-minute panic dash to locate all the items she has brought with her, which seem to have randomly found themselves in highly obscure places. I have an entire drawer of her forgotten items – Christmas cards she came over to collect and then left without remembering, a vape charger, jewellery, scrunchies, lipsticks... Then all of a sudden in a Stevie Nicks haze of floaty scarves and nice perfume smells (she always smells so clean, which is one of my favourite things about her) she scoops her kitchen sinks into her oversized bag and vanishes into the night.

I pour myself another vino tinto and muster up courage for our next session. I've got this. I can do it. It's time for Veronica to get in the bin.

HOW TO READ THE DANGER SIGNS

So by now we understand all about some of the potential pitfalls we can fall into when it comes to communication, but what are some of the red flags we need to look out for in terms of the actual therapist? Perhaps a little naïve of me, but generally I believe that most therapists and social workers gravitate towards the caring professions because they have a desire to help others. One bad experience in therapy doesn't mean they will all be and like the world of dating; sometimes you have to kiss a lot of frogs to find a prince (him/her/them).

I'm keen to get away from any attribution of blame in this chapter, therapists aren't super-humans and we don't know what we don't know. In psychology terms we refer to this as being consciously incompetent where we don't know how to do something (yet) but are willing to learn. However, due to the very nature of the inherent power dynamic in the therapist–client relationship there are sadly a great deal of clinicians assuming the role of all-knowing expert as if their own studies override the client's perception.

I have worked with countless individuals who have experienced significant harm in therapy because they were invalidated and not believed – their visible distress being taken as evidence of their defensiveness (lose-lose situation). We may be told that we are unconsciously hiding, which is possibly the worst gaslighting state-ment you could use on an autistic person aligning with values such as truth, fairness and justice.

If we're the type of autistic person to struggle with picking up on signs and signals, how on earth do we know if we're in the path of harm? In my experience there are a few types of therapist we might want to swerve if we are to ensure our mental health is not damaged in the healing process.

Whilst it might not be obvious when we first meet someone (especially not from reading their online profile or having an introductory consultation where they may be on their best behaviour), over time you should be able to start noticing patterns in their conduct. Something which I think it's fair to say we're all pretty good at!.

If you feel the relationship is generally solid, reliable and trustworthy but feel that one comment made you feel uncomfortable, make a note of it and see if anything like that happens again. If you feel safe to do so, try getting feedback from people you can trust. Therapists are human beings and bound to make mistakes, but it's how it's dealt with that really matters. If you decide to raise your concern with them, how do they respond? Does it feel healthy and respectful, or do you feel that you've been told off, put down and shamed? So with that said, watch out for the following types:

- The misattuned therapist
- The autism denier
- The minimizer
- The 'I'm right' therapist
- The bad listener

The misattuned therapist

It seems like every week I meet someone who has been on the wrong end of a therapist's dodgy hypothesis of an unconscious conflict and point blank refusing to accept they're wrong. Recently a friend of mine shared how their being nice in therapy (because they didn't see any reason to be in an ill-tempered mood!) seemed to aggravate her counsellor who accused them of being passive-aggressive. My friend felt deeply attacked as this couldn't be further from her truth, but her therapist refused to let it go.

Some people are just nice. We can't be in sync all the time but it is important in therapy to feel that your therapist is at least trying to stay in your frame of reference. In terms of red flags do you get the impression they are irritated by you or frustrated? Do you feel belittled or that you can't get anything 'right'? Does your therapist scoff or mock you? Do you feel safe in correcting them or does it seem they must have the final say? An emerging pattern could indicate that there is something seriously amiss in the dynamic.

'The therapist I was referred to was a behavioural therapist for supposed social anxiety, but we would often end up in an argument. I'd already tried so many of the things he suggested and he was insistent that I just try harder. When it became too overwhelming I would go non-verbal which isn't something I have any control over. He even accused me of lying, making things more difficult than they really are, and essentially being overly dramatic. I would leave his office in tears. Eventually he told me I was clearly unwilling to engage in therapy and dismissed me. Now I've found a new therapist but am terrified it will go the exact same way. It's left me with some deep scars and abandonment issues.'

The autism denier ('It's all in your head, excuses, excuses')

Many of the clients I work with arrive at my office deeply hurt because a former therapist or mental health practitioner has accused them of using suspected autism (or a self-diagnosis) as an avoidance strategy for 'doing the work'. I firmly believe that if an individual finds the courage to utter the statement, 'I think I might be neurodivergent', it is essential to treat this with the same levels of non-judgemental empathy, trust, respect and curiosity as we would with a client who tells us they think they're gay.

It isn't the job of a therapist to try and disprove others, only to help people understand themselves better and draw their own conclusions. It worries me that for some of us our initial spark of awareness might be snuffed out by dismissive therapists who think they know what autism looks like when their clinical knowledge is limited to low-masking autistics.

'I was told my issues were a basic lack of social skills and throughout my session the therapist kept mocking me, mirroring my body language and facial expressions as if to draw these things to my attention. It was horrible. She treated me as if I were a total idiot that needed to learn some kind of hard lesson. I felt no warmth or compassion from her but just assumed that was what therapy was like with nothing to draw from.'

The minimizer ('We're all a bit autistic')

If I had a pound for every time I hear this statement I could probably retire to a nice beach hut in Bora Bora. It's not that the majority of people necessarily mean anything bad when they say this, and in many cases it's their clumsy way of finding commonality. The reality is that this can feel seriously undermining and trivializing, particularly if said by someone entrusted to a position of power.

The thing is that autistic traits are human traits and just because you happen to like routine, or find jumpers itchy, or like a nice neat spice jar cupboard does not make someone autistic! However, if someone ticks **all** of the diagnostic trait boxes then you might wish to counter that statement with, 'Have you looked into getting a diagnosis?!'

'My therapist told me that I can't be autistic because I've got a husband, a job and can do eye-contact well. When I explained I'd been learning all about how the condition presents in women he told me not to believe everything I read on the internet, and that it's all mentally ill people convincing themselves they're neurodivergent in an attempt to avoid dealing with their real problems. I stayed with that therapist for another few months because I felt he knew better than me.'

The 'I'm right' therapist (God)

There are always going to be grandiose, pompous and bombastic people in life who believe they are right (and you are wrong). Amassing a wodge of credentials doesn't mean you have 'dealt' with your stuff or even have the self-awareness to explore your shadow characteristics. One of the things I'm very keen on is dismantling the concept of 'therapist as expert', as if somehow we are infallible and above experiencing challenges in life.

I notice how this type of therapist doesn't really want clients, they want groupies and adoration – someone to stroke their ego and make them feel worthy. There's nothing wrong with looking up to your therapist as a sort of role model, but it's crucial that the therapist doesn't try and create an image that they are somehow perfect.

I once wrote an article about the importance of lived experience working in the field of psychology, prompted by a column I'd read where a therapist (who trained after his retirement) declared that he'd 'never needed therapy' (Jones 2018). I remember feeling appalled by this statement as though there were well people and mentally unwell people. Ask yourself whether you feel really seen by your therapist. Are they empathizing with you the best they can? Do they summarize your words back to you with accuracy or does it feel like it's a space for them to flex their knowledge?

The problem with egotistical, self-absorbed, arrogant types is that they tend to lack the ability to notice these qualities within themselves. They demand a certain level of complicity from others to make up for the fact that they are hideously insecure beneath the surface. But the real issue for this type of therapist is that they aren't open to constructive feedback (whether from a client or their own supervisor). In their own minds they are right and it's everyone else who is beneath them.

Individuals with dark triad personalities (narcissism, psychopathy and Machiavellianism) thrive in all areas of society, particularly in those where they can assume a position of authority, influence and attention.

Exercise caution, ask about their supervision process (they need to be in supervision!) and if you feel comfortable doing so (perhaps even anonymously on an online forum) check out if their behaviour is received by others in the same way you feel. It's easy to doubt yourself in such a vulnerable position and sometimes a second opinion is worth a lot of wasted time, money and restricted growth.

The bad listener

As practitioners we are trained in something called 'active listening', which is a bit different from your average day-to-day conversation. With active listening we are expected to pay careful attention not just to what is being said (the words) but also the tone, delivery, body language, facial expressions, contradictions, hesitancies, and so on, in order to synthesize, reflect and feedback our understanding to clients. Some people can do this naturally and don't require much in the way of skilling-up during their psych training. However, there are also those who, well, suck at it quite frankly.

As autistic people we're used to dealing with lots of information when we communicate, often comfortably monologuing back and forth with a friend. Many neurotypicals on the other hand tend to deal in sound bites and fill in the gaps themselves, often becoming lost in the types of dialogue that feel organic to us.

I remember one therapist who only managed to retain the first few things I said in an info dump – all of it felt relevant to catch her up to speed. This was brought to my attention by her asking me questions about things I'd already mentioned. When I'm working with a client I remember everything they have ever told me (not a brag, that's just how my brain works) but clearly this isn't how the average neurotypical brain operates.

If you feel you are frequently misunderstood in your sessions, lectured (particularly given unsolicited advice), asked to repeat yourself often, or feel your therapist is muddling up your story (perhaps even confusing you with someone else!), listen to that inner concern. If there's one place we need to feel seen and heard, it's the therapy room.

HOW WE MAY BE HARMED

The following list is not exhaustive by any means – it seems as though I hear a new horror story every day about when therapy has gone wrong. One of the problems is that harm is difficult to quantify as it's a largely subjective experience. For some, a negative experience might be that it made them feel a little low for a while. For others, the aftermath of bad therapy might be completely devastating.

A 2016 study by Crawford et al. examined data from 14,500 respondents who had engaged in NHS psychological services and found that 5% experienced lasting negative outcomes. I dread to think what the rate would be if we could filter out all the neurodivergent individuals (particularly those of us who are undiagnosed and misdiagnosed) and would like to see more research carried out in this area. Here are a few examples of how we might be harmed and things to look out for:

- feeling blamed and shamed
- being accused of 'client resistance' or being 'difficult' – the therapist not owning **their** feelings of frustration and powerlessness at our lack of progress (taking it personally and expressing it as anger towards you)
- receiving invalidation
- gaslighting
- being humiliated and ridiculed
- being judged
- being undermined
- boundary violations (this may include inappropriate discussions, trying to establish a relationship outside of sessions, physical or sexual advances)
- being silenced
- unresolved conflict in the therapeutic relationship
- being accused of emotional blackmail/attention-seeking
- not feeling seen
- being controlled or dominated in sessions
- having goals misunderstood or therapist having different goals
- being encouraged to take a course of action which ultimately causes harm (suggesting they leave a relationship or job)
- being encouraged to mask as 'best social behaviour' (suppression of self) and something we 'all have to do'

- therapist not understanding that typical relaxation techniques may not work for us and expressing exasperation.

There is also the concern that therapy might not be the best option for the client but the therapist needs to feel worthy and valuable (retaining clients for financial/personal gain).

At the end of this book we will explore the antidote to these behaviours and provide helpful tips from the autistic community in terms of how neuro-affirming practitioners can better adapt to our needs and ensure we get the best support possible. It's also worth noting that if you are a professional and can identify with any of these behaviours that you don't beat yourself over the head with a big stick. We are **all** in a constant state of learning – what I know about autism today will be a tiny fraction of what I know in five years' time. As human beings we learn best from making mistakes.

An autistic friend of mine told me how a past therapist had once accused her of emotional blackmail around her self-harming. She had gone to great lengths to conceal this from her family out of embarrassment and in hindsight could see that her self-injurious behaviour was actually symptomatic of autistic meltdowns due to mounting pressures. He kept going on at her, demanding she admit it, and claiming that she knew exactly what she was doing. My friend told me that she was in such an upset state she couldn't find the words to express herself and felt that she was being told off by a headmaster.

'The damage done to me at the hands of my ex therapist left me with a burning rage of injustice for many years – not to be believed is one thing (and bad enough!) but to have your intentions completely taken out of context and reflected back to you as though you are manipulative is quite another.'

Professor Tony Attwood reflects on how many neurotypical therapists can be too academic in their approach:

It's too much mind and not enough heart, and psychology and counselling is as much an art as it is a science. I tell colleagues to suspend all previous conceptions and learn from the client. Trust is essential. You've got to be able to understand things from their perspective – what is realistic and what is not? I think in a way this is an issue of personality and attitude independent of professional training. Many clinicians are working with their cognition – 'how does this fit into my understanding of neurology?' – expecting clients to fit into their framework, rather than seeing them as a unique person and working on issues together.

Tony's comment makes me think about how we teach this to new trainees, since much of what he is describing is around having compassion and empathy. Unfortunately (particularly in mental health services with fixed numbers of sessions) the goals for the client will typically be around demonstrating an **improvement** (not fixed, not healed, just improved) in a particular problematic area. For example, by your final session it is hoped that you will score lower on anxiety and depression markers than when you started.

Within modalities such as cognitive behavioural therapy there may be a specific challenge to complete – if someone has social anxiety they may have a goal to make a new friend and work towards this incrementally. However, real personal growth takes time and the confines of a safe strong relationship to test things out.

Therapists who see multiple patients a week (30+) may not find it all that easy to really 'lock into' a person and develop that kind of deep soul connection, given that they are working under pressure within a time-limited parameter. They may favour more of a solution-focused 'quick win' approach, which might not provide us with the kinds of skills and resources we can easily transfer to other areas of our lives. One therapist I had in my early twenties decided that my 'task' was to say how I felt to a person I fancied, completely overlooking everything that had happened in my life to make me wary of others.

For me the journey to compassion, empathy and radical acceptance is far from formulaic and needs careful training which recognizes the heart, mind and spirit – we are not algorithms.

Any of us can make mistakes but it's how we fix them that's important. I can't help but feel I've probably caused accidental harm in my own career and sometimes worry about a time where I had to take unexpected time off due to a severe autistic burnout. What was the impact on those clients? Did they feel abandoned? Rejected? Angry? Let down? I am incredibly grateful to the following neurodivergent therapist who wanted to anonymously share their worries about failing a former client:

> I once had a client with a history of sexual abuse and so met criteria for complex PTSD based on what happened. It actually took me over a year to identify that she also met criteria for autism, since her avoidant and hypervigilant behaviours did seem related to trauma. It was challenging because she

related the behaviours to her trauma (avoidance of crowds, anxiety around speaking to new people, needing a lot of alone time, only interacting with friends through video games because going out felt exhausting, and feeling over-whelmed by loud noises and sensory stimuli). At one point I felt very frustrated with her because it seemed like she was victimizing herself by blaming her abuse history for her inability to do things like hold a full-time job or maintain relationships. I would say some of my own ableism got in the way too. I now realize that she seemed stuck because she was in the wrong environments and I was looking at the wrong issues. I only figured it out after I had finally been diagnosed myself.

This really echoes my own experiences in the therapy room, and whilst I'm certainly not blaming myself here, or any therapist (you don't know what you don't know), the reality is that we're very unlikely to bring other helpful clues into sessions if we don't deem it relative to the narrative we already hold. I would never have thought to mention I have certain food aversions (get away from me eggs, you evil things!) or that I go to pieces if I end up with a sticky hand whilst I'm out and about. The majority of my special interests tend to be things that others might even consider main-stream – certain bands, TV shows, films – but it's really about the power of the intensity rather than the topic itself. Why on earth would I mention that I listened to Queens of the Stoneage for an entire year on repeat because it just 'felt good'?

I once read somewhere that if you train to be a therapist you should write off the first ten years as **practice**. A comment like that doesn't really fill you with all that much confidence in the psychological professionals but, like Tony mentioned before, therapy is as much an art as it is a science. It can be incredibly difficult to figure out the different elements with neurodivergent clients, but when it happens and the penny drops, it is hugely beneficial for both parties.

RED HERRINGS

So let's take a quick look at what we might be saying (at face value!) and how this might possibly be (mis)interpreted by our therapist. I can only hope that this list finds itself on the desk of every psychological trainee so that they may suspend their judgements and be open to the possibility of something else going on behind the scenes. Consider this your neurodivergent to neurotypical Google translation!

Therapist interpretation	Autistic person's reality
Obsessions	Special interests
Egotistical/self-absorbed	Talkative/wanting to be understood, unable to notice when another person is uninterested in what they are saying
Paranoia	Social confusion and hyper-awareness
Avoidance	Social preferences (enjoys being alone) or not being sure how to make/maintain friendships
Narcissistic ('So you think you're special?')	Identifying sense of feeling different and trying to understand what that means (also self-identifying particular hyper-skills and cognitive strengths interpreted as 'being better' than others)
Multiple personality disorder	Masking/social performance
Emotionally unstable/having tantrums/out of control	Autistic meltdowns

Dissociation	Autistic shutdown, involuntary sensory break, overwhelm, sessions moving too fast to keep up/take in information
Compliance in therapy (lack of agency)	Masking/people-pleasing response due to not knowing who the unmasked version of themselves is
Seen as going off on tangents – giving irrelevant content to deflect/avoid talking about 'the real issues'	Fear of missing out an important piece, everything feels connected, detail-orientated thinking style
Resistance/denial when a client says 'I don't know'	Alexithymia, unclear on feelings, needing extra time to process, executive dysfunction, preference for intellectual analysis over feelings not clinically regarded as acceptable
Not listening	Problems in processing verbal data/ instructions, social confusion, or deeply listening but not giving the expected affirmative body language
Schizophrenia/magical thinking/severe mental illness/hallucinations	Hyper-intuition, pattern-spotting, signs and synchronicities, hyper-awareness, hyper-empathy, synaesthesia
Disproportionate reactions (over-reactions perceived as histrionic, under-reaction perceived as not being in touch with self/emotionally stunted)	Hypo-/hyper-sensitivities
Neurotic/controlling/ obsessive	High moral values, spotting small mistakes, needing routines, predictability, safety and systems
Lack of co-operation (in session or homework)	Overwhelmed/can't cope (too much to do) – even turning up to a session each week may feel incredibly draining
Refusal to speak in session – power play/regressive behaviour/arrested development/petulance/ sulking	Gone non-verbal due to being overstimulated and unable to find words to express oneself adequately, not clear on expectations, fear

cont.

Therapist interpretation	Autistic person's reality
Observable signs of anxiety	Soothing stimming behaviours
Self-pity/victim mentality	Realities of being a neurodivergent person in a neurotypical world
Assumed lack of self-awareness/ego defences	Difficulty bridging the double empathy problem/being understood
Splitting	Black-and-white thinking
Histrionic personality	Catastrophizing
Rebelling against authority	Autonomy, unconventional life choices and interests
Evasive eye-contact (perceived as shifty)	Struggles with holding eye-contact due to autonomic nervous system overstimulation
Cognitive errors in thinking	Natural thinking patterns of autistic person
Rigidity, unwillingness, resistance to change	Underlying struggles with adapting/transitioning to new sensory environments; assimilation of new systems processes without adequate time to update our inner mind map causing deep anxiety; change without support can be traumatic; executive dysfunction meaning we cannot execute the changes required
Childish behaviour/immature (judged as non-age appropriate)	Child-like curiosity, unconventional interests, a playfulness not conditioned out of us by society, may appear much younger than we chronologically are
Hypochondria, psychosomatic illness, stress	Acute sensitivity to internal sensations not typically felt by others; such changes may trigger a panic response
Depression or 'tired all the time'	Autistic burnout/fatigue, slow motor-skill response (e.g. movement/speech) due to natural capacity being exceeded
Self-harm	Self-injurious behaviour in an attempt to self-regulate or communicate, often occurring at the point of meltdown

Samantha Stein (Yo Samdy Sam), author and YouTuber shares:

Before I was diagnosed (so unable to identify sensory stuff) you just try and explain it away and end up coming up with a completely different answer than if you understood your own sensory needs. Maybe it was super, super loud all day. Maybe you met a lot of people. Maybe there were people jostling and bumping into you all day. So all these things have been building up but you're attributing it to an incident it's not even about. And if you're in a situation where a therapist doesn't understand that, they're also going to be guiding you to reach a different conclusion about the situation and ultimately about yourself.

It's only been a few years since I was diagnosed and I'm still trying to work out who I really am based on the half-stories I created in therapy. Anger has always been a big part of my life, which I assumed was to do with my mother's temper. However, as I start to peel back the layers I notice more often than not it's just an unmet need making itself known.

Perhaps I'm hungry (but received no alert from my stomach), maybe I'm thirsty (and haven't drunk all day), could it be that I'm just tired and interpreting it as irritable feelings? As a child when I was deeply upset I would often hysterically cry out, 'No one gets it, I want to go home,' much to the confusion of my mother who would scream back, 'But you **are** home, you're in your bedroom.' If only I had the knowledge and language to communicate what I was really trying to say: 'I recognize that I am different to other people, doing the same things as them is exponentially difficult for me somehow, and I am desperate to be around like-minded others because feeling misunderstood is fucking soul destroying.'

SUMMARY

- The danger signs in therapy are important to learn to spot. These include misattunement, invalidation, minimization, grandiosity and poor listening.
- There are many ways we may experience harm in therapy, for example blame, shame and ridicule.
- It is important to bring the totality of ourselves into sessions, not just what has harmed us, but what we enjoy too, so that the therapist may listen out for indications that we are autistic.
- If we already know we are autistic, we should guard against attempts to condition us out of our traits because our behaviours are perceived as abnormal.
- There may be big differences between how therapists interpret our behaviour and what we actually mean.

Chapter 6

THERAPEUTIC CONCEPTS

Sitting on the plastic chair outside Veronica's room feels terrifying today, it's as if time has slowed down, I can't breathe properly and my eyesight has become laser sharp. I attempt calming positive self-talk in my head, 'There is literally no need to be scared, she is a professional. There won't be any drama or conflict, in fact she'll probably be pleased that you're ready to end.'

Bang on cue her vampiric portcullis swings open and her forced smile drags me inside.

As I wriggle around in my (still cockeyed) chair Veronica leans forward to reach for her coffee, taking a sip without so much as breaking eye-contact with me. I have a dreadful sinking feeling that there is going to be some kind of showdown, as if speaking your mind is a crime round these parts, but the truth is I'm done, I can't stand being in her presence a moment longer. I take a long deep breath. Here goes nothing.

'So basically, Veronica, I've given it some considerable thought and I've decided that this just isn't working out for me. It's been well over a year now and to be honest I feel worse than I've ever felt. It's like talking through stuff isn't giving me any new insight or fresh ways forward, instead I'm just drowning. There's nothing new under the sun to explore, just rumination and **thinking** isn't solving any of my problems.'

Veronica, nods her head slowly. Maybe I've got her all wrong! She seems supportive!

'This is the most authentic I've ever seen you, Steph.'

Oh God, I was wrong all along!! She was just trying to help! I knew I'd misinterpreted it all. Typical me. Why do I assume the worst in people who are there to care for me?!

'And', she continued, 'I think that you're creating conflict to avoid the pain of our sessions finishing.'

Sorry, what now? Not only is she not taking me at face value but she is trying to twist my words to imply I am secretly in denial of my feelings. How on earth can this woman think in her heart that she means that much to me? It's so beyond narcissistic I can hardly take it in.

What. The. Actual. Fuck.

I am suddenly hit by the disturbing revelation that if I start to explain **why** I don't like her, why I think sessions are a waste of time and money, and quite frankly why I'd rather have all my teeth extracted without a local anaesthetic, she will only hear that as further evidence of my deep feelings in her warped, conceited and egotistical mind. This is so messed up.

'Veronica, the truth is I've had my reservations about this particular approach for a while, it just doesn't feel like it's helping and from talking to my professional peers they tend to agree that we're just not a good fit.'

'But you've been coming to sessions for **a year** and didn't think to mention this **before?**' Her tone is clipped as if she's caught me in a lie.

'Quite honestly I find the blank screen thing really uncomfortable, conversation doesn't flow naturally, you don't seem to 'get me' at all and I don't feel you're on my side. With other therapists in the past I've felt supported, like we're a team. But with you what I'm trying to say is that as a client with a history of trauma I find your approach deliberately antagonistic and damaging.' I feel so proud of myself.

Veronica laughs loudly down her nose and screws up her face as if she's just drunk a pint of vinegar. Did my therapist actually just laugh at me?

'Okay, Stephanie, I think we're done here. Enough is enough. S-T-O-P', she shouts leaning forward in her chair, eye-balling me and raising her right hand in an extremely aggressive manner.

The fact that **she** is accusing **me** of being aggressive whilst raising her voice, going red in the face, shutting me down with a hand gesture, practically hyper-ventilating and sweating through her pale blue shirt tells me she is a total hypocrite. From her over-the-top response you'd think I had physically attacked her. For a split second I wonder if she is the one who will miss me. Have I triggered some rejection wound in her? What the hell is going on and where's that sparrow when you need him?

During this whole fiasco not only am I imagining what this must look like to someone looking in, but I am also relating it to how I behave as a therapist. In almost ten years of practice I have never so much as raised my voice to a client. In my opinion voicing a concern in a therapeutic session is something to be celebrated – it takes real guts to find your courage. It's as if she can't see **me** at all. Instead she's fixed on her interpretation that I am re-enacting some kind of early trauma. Aren't I just asserting my boundaries? Isn't that what we help clients to create?

Despite having one foot in reality, the very nature of this exchange and the power dynamic held firmly in her favour leads me to question myself. Am I just distorting what's going on here? Did I do something wrong? Am I so messed up that I'm actually just having some kind of psychotic episode and aren't even aware of it? This is the very nature of gaslighting, it fills the target with cognitive dissonance.

As the self-doubt roars around my brain I see a crystal-clear vision of all my friends, my family, clients, colleagues and acquaintances throughout the years standing before me. I see that the altercation I have found myself in is a one-off event, it is not a pattern, nobody else feels this way towards me and this has not happened before. The trauma of the situation has made my body feel like lead, my head filled with a kind of white static that temporarily disables my thoughts. I feel small, vulnerable and afraid. I **am** in danger. Something very bad is happening.

All of a sudden a beautiful feeling of protection wraps around me and my senses click into sharp focus. I hear a voice from somewhere deep inside which says, 'Now, get up, leave and never look back.' It was such a profound experience and to be honest I'm not entirely sure that voice belonged to me. I got to my feet and picked up my bag.

'I'm leaving now.'

Still visibly shaken she tossed her hair around several times and started rubbing her right earlobe in a sort of pathetic and petulant attempt to gain the upper hand. Only there was no upper hand to be gained, this ordeal was over. She snarled, 'Yes, I agree, I think you'd better go. And I think it will be very helpful to analyse this in some considerable detail next week, it could prove very damaging to your progress to end things like this.'

As I close the door behind me I recognize her for what she really is – a menacing, sadistic, insecure bully who cannot bear to be criticized. Calling out her professional competence was too much for her to deal with and rather than admit her failings it was easier to redirect the blame, perceive herself as a victim, and project all her disowned negative characteristics onto me. I will later learn all about 'altruistic narcissists' who view themselves as perfect caregivers and demand others collude with their self-concept.

Back at my car, I get in, slump back in my chair and pull down the visor mirror. I feel okay but my eyes tell a different story, their usual light blue turning a shade of gunmetal. I do not feel any compulsion to scream or shout or cry, but there is a new sensation within me which I can only describe as a white hot seriousness. In that moment I am unable to correctly identify just how traumatic that situation was or recognize what long-lasting effect it will have on me. Always operating at a pragmatic, logical level, I figure it's done, over. Nothing left to see here, people, I'm driving home now.

How absolutely wrong I was.

As I flick through my various manuals and textbooks, I get to thinking about how many of the approaches, concepts, theories and techniques could seriously damage a neurodivergent mind and wonder why there isn't more written about this topic.

Only this morning I was reading an article about self-help strategies which encouraged people to just 'try harder' when faced with difficult times. Push on, keep going, you've got this! The cynic in me feels that society really just wants us all to be extroverted capitalists, slaying it at the office 12 hours a day, then spending your hard-earned wages on partying hard (work hard, play hard, bro!). It's the kind of life that breaks so many of us and simply isn't something we can maintain long-term without losing other bits of your life through compensation.

A better approach in my view would be to carry out a compassionate inventory of where we're at, identifying the resources and capacity we have and working within our energy window – working smarter, not harder. When I look back at my life, all the achievements I'm supposed to feel **proudest** of or feel **excited** about are simply dark and traumatic times I'd rather forget. Most of those experiences have resulted in significant autistic meltdowns, episodes of self-harm and suicidal ideation. I only wish I could go back and comfort that poor young woman driving herself to the brink. But what other psychological theories and strategies might not translate to the neurodivergent experience?

PSYCHOLOGICAL THEORIES

Reframing

Cognitive reframing is a very popular technique which helps (most) people to change the way they think about things. One of my clients shared how reframing in sessions with another therapist made her not trust her instincts by essentially denying the reality of her internal experience. Being optimistic, whilst generally a good attitude to have, isn't going to magic away the very real social and sensory issues we face born with a neurological difference.

That said, some of my clients find it very helpful to recognize that they are actually catastrophizing and imagining a worst-case scenario which is worsening their anxiety, and together we will come up with a counter-balance thought ('actually what is the **best-case** scenario that might happen?') to help defuse the distressing thoughts. None of us can predict the future. Well, maybe Mystic Meg.

Graded exposure

Graded exposure is a way of helping people overcome certain fears by allowing them to become desensitized (over a period of time) to the thing causing them distress. For example a phobia of snakes, spiders or flying. This process (called habituation) serves to reduce anxiety in many neurotypicals but does not take into account our basic neurology.

Professor Tony Attwood explains: 'As in sensory sensitivity, repeated exposure does not reduce the reaction. In fact repeated exposure (which you get in rumination) actually consolidates it and makes it worse.'

I'm all for everyone pushing through our comfort zones as much as possible in the name of growth but we also need to be careful that we're not just trying to push our neurodivergent brains into a neurotypical mindset.

Window of tolerance

Similar to the above, the widow of tolerance is a concept developed by Dr. Dan Siegel (2015). He talks about the optimum state of arousal for a person to function effectively. It might be helpful to imagine three layers stacked on top of each other for this explanation. In the middle layer – the preferable zone – we feel grounded, flexible, open and able to self-regulate easily. The top layer above this is the hyper-arousal zone – these kind of feelings might include anger, overwhelm, high energy, hyper-vigilance and tension; and finally the bottom layer being that of hypo-arousal, indicated by feeling depressed, shutdown, frozen, withdrawn and passive.

In therapy the goal is to try and expand the middle layer by encouraging clients to 'sit in the distress', which may not be all that effective when our neurobiology affects our ability to acclimatize. Personally I think of my own window of tolerance as a faulty boiler which doesn't switch off when it overheats. Sitting in distress is likely to exacerbate the pain, and a far better approach would be to remove yourself from any situation or person triggering such a reaction in you.

Attachment theory

Between the 1930s and 1950s the British psychologist John Bowlby began creating a theory based on his observations of orphans and emotionally distressed children. Bowlby believed that children are born with a kind of automatic drive to attach in order to aid their survival. He felt that our earliest relationships with our parents creates a type of interaction blueprint (or attachment style) for the rest of our lives. As the theory goes, the more secure and stable our initial relationships with our early caregivers, the more confident we will feel to explore the world as we grow.

In the 1940s the Austrian Psychiatrist Leo Kanner (who published the first description of early autism in children) decided that autism was the result of unavailable and uncaring mothers who had essentially traumatized their child into being autistic. Bruno Bettelheim (an Austrian-born American psychologist and a student of Freud) subsequently built on this idea and Bettelheim's theory of autism (also known as the 'refrigerator mother theory') floated around until it was later proven to be absolute crap. (One of his treatments was to remove autistic children from their poor parents, I can't even imagine.)

Autism is a neurodevelopmental condition and has nothing, precisely diddly squat, to do with the way you were raised. Difficulties in communication and socializing may look like some kind of attachment disorder (usually insecure/anxious) in therapy, but this is why it's so important for clinicians to be open-minded to the possibility of autism with this kind of presentation.

THERAPEUTIC STRATEGIES

The therapeutic dialogue (mirroring, paraphrasing, reflection)

The typical flow of a therapy session (whilst different for everyone) is built around a neurotypical communication style of back and forth conversation, with the therapist occasionally pausing the client to check their understanding and reflect that back. Unfortunately for many of us this kind of interruption can be very jarring, disorientating and seem pointless and artificial. It may not serve us to have someone take up **our** session time with **their** thoughts on what we have just said if our primary goal is to release our negative energy and externally process (the famous info dump).

We may also need longer to think about what a therapist says so that we can process how it might be relevant, yet many therapists may misconstrue our silence as containing a deeper meaning. Professor Tony Attwood described how his psychotherapist colleague Rachel Harris (also autistic) has devised her own therapy which incorporates and values silence to enable neurodivergent clients to go 'offline' and really think about what is being said without the pressure of having to engage in conventional interactions.

Body language

In the early 1970s Albert Mehrabian (a researcher of body language) declared that during face-to-face conversations, 55% of how we communicate is non-verbal, 38% is vocal (tone, how we say it) and only 7% is the words themselves (Mehrabian 1971). But much of the psychological training around body language simply won't apply to autistic people if our tone, facial expressions or gestures do not communicate our inner feelings in a predictable way most neurotypical people understand.

As therapists we are trained to look out for incongruences between what someone says and how they say it. We are taught that evading eye-contact is a sign of deception, denial or anxiety. Personally in my practice I have thrown out much of what I know about body language when it comes to neurodivergent clients, we have our own ways of communicating and it's important to **trust** the person sitting before us. (I am often told I sound insincere when I'm actually really happy for someone, leading me to work on my performance in front of a mirror at home!)

Therapeutic ruptures

Communication breakdowns are a fact of life. Like everything that happens in the outside world, patterns, themes and dynamics will eventually get re-enacted in the therapeutic relationship. According to research when 'good enough' therapists correctly detect and actively work with ruptures it may be one of the most transformational growth-promoting experiences in the treatment (Safran et al. 2001).

However, many of us may find it impossible to re-connect with our therapist after we feel there has been a wrongdoing of sorts. Our polarized thinking patterns, sense of justice and sensitivity to others' negative qualities make it very difficult to see them in a positive light after trust has broken down.

FLEXIBILITY IS THE KEY

It is absolutely critical that anyone working in therapy holds a basic understanding of how many of the foundational concepts and theories simply do not align with our neurology. Therapists should remain open and flexible to considering alternative approaches which avoid a typical 'client-must-fit-framework' compliance.

I am encouraged that many modalities often have adaptations when it comes to working with neurodivergence. However, I'm still very much from the philosophy that therapy for autistic people should be devised **by** neurodivergent therapists and service-users. That said, could you confidently state at this point that you know what you need in therapy? Do you feel you understand how it all works and the kinds of accommodations you could ask for? It takes a confident person to assert themselves, but if we don't feel 'in the know' we're unlikely to be able to carry ourselves with enough internal power to get what we want.

The next chapter looks at how we can become that informed, knowledgeable therapee so we start to make informed decisions about our own wellbeing, and not be at the mercy of someone who doesn't understand us **and** assumes they know best. Let's make sure we're choosing the right kinds of therapy and the right kind of therapist...

SUMMARY

- Many psychological concepts and theories in traditional therapies are simply not transferable when it comes to working with autistic clients.
- Similarly the way therapy is conducted is often less suitable for neurodivergent clients.
- Such approaches may be at best ineffective and at worst distressing.

Chapter 7

CHOOSING THE RIGHT THERAPY AND THERAPIST

Despite feeling initially better after ending sessions with Veronica, relieved I guess, for months afterwards I am caught in spiralling ruminations and intrusive thoughts. I find myself waking in the middle of the night re-playing all the various snippets of our time together and reflecting on how utterly horrendous the experience really was. Why was I so naïve? Why did I literally pay this person to make me feel like crap, and what the hell is actually wrong with me?

I sob on my boyfriend's shoulder until his clean white T-shirt is covered with mascara (again). It's an all-too-familiar scene for him, I seem to collapse in snotty puddles of Steph all over the place and appear to have cultivated the resilience of a new born kitten. I didn't use to feel this bad even before I went to therapy and without running the risk of sounding melodramatic I feel **violated**.

Veronica was my ninth therapist since my mid-twenties, surely at least one of them would have been able to help me enough so that life doesn't feel completely unmanageable. It makes no sense to me, I seem to do well in certain areas – like my career

– but fall on my arse when it comes to remembering to brush my teeth or how to cook a meal. Some days I can't recall simple things like how to make a cup of tea, and I'm terrified I'm losing my marbles. Mike (the boyfriend) has commented that he can tell when I'm not doing great because I start to stutter and punch myself in the head in frustration. Am I mad? Do I need to be locked away?

Looking in the mirror I start to worry that maybe I am mad, I'm going grey and getting wrinkles. Maybe I'm turning into a crazy cat lady. The thought of this also makes me start to cry. It's like the harder I push the worse things get and I have this inner feeling which tells me I'm not living life as I'm supposed to – but what does that even mean?

The whole thing makes me feel like an impostor in my work – how can I be a good therapist and assist my clients to feel better when I can't do that for myself? Why are they getting better under my care but anything I try for myself (and trust me I'm fresh out of ideas) doesn't work? If I have one more doctor telling me I'm depressed and just need to do more exercise, I swear to God I will ram their stethoscope up their backsides.

Months go by in a kind of blur until one day a letter comes through the door from the mental health team. I've been on the waiting list for EMDR (eye movement desensitization and reprocessing) for so long I totally forgot about it and feel a little more than apprehensive to start again with another stranger. Surely it can't get any worse, can it?

One Thursday afternoon I show up at my appointment time and sit nervously in a big waiting room full of people talking far too loudly. What on earth do they find to talk about? People make conversation seem so effortless, it's as if they're not even thinking about it. From around a light-pink painted corner a smiley man appears and calls out my name in a cheerful way, which reminds me of a TV game show host. His name is Stephen. Unlike Veronica he has a warm and kind manner about him and frequently makes jokes, which I like. I can tell he isn't interested in being on an ego trip and doesn't come across as bored, superior or patronizing.

'I'm really worried about being here truth be told, I've just had a horrific experience with a psychodynamic therapist and the whole thing has left me scarred. I just can't seem to let it go, the audacity of upsetting a client and then not taking any responsibility. I even wrote her a letter describing how badly I was doing and all I got back was a one-line email saying, I hope you feel better for sharing this and that you can now move on. It's like there's no consequences to her actions, no accountability, no apology, no understanding... where's her humanity?'

'Well, she wouldn't apologize, would she? Those kinds of therapists are **never** wrong. It's in their God-like training to blame everyone else.'

I think I had secretly expected Stephen to side with her but in him calling out poor practice I felt so seen. It was as if the simple act of him saying 'yes, that really was out of line and you didn't deserve it' went a long way to healing the hurt. It felt a little bit magical actually. I feel so relaxed in our sessions together as he sits across from me sipping his mug of tea and apologizing for slurping too loudly. It feels **real**. Even when there's a misunderstanding, we work through it, there's no conflict or drama – I feel safe.

Back in my office, one serendipitous afternoon I was seeing my client Jannine, who gave her permission for me to tell her story in this book. Jannine is an incredible woman so full of passion, intelligence, sharp humour and self-awareness. I always looked forward to our sessions and valued how honest and deep she was. Although I loved working with Jannine I didn't feel like I was helping her all that much to be honest, and all the trauma techniques in my toolkit seemed to be hitting brick walls. A bit like with me and my moods, there was often no reason or rhyme to her ups and downs, often described as huge melt-downs which required days of recovery. Bursting through my door and almost out of breath due to some issues with the 328 bus, Jannine got comfortable on my tatty old sofa and poured herself a glass of water.

'How are you do-ing?!' I asked, not really in a therapist kind of way but more as a like-minded soul who hadn't seen their friend in a while. I feel less like a therapist with Jannine but don't know why.

'Oh! Steph! Steph! I mean! I don't even know where to begin on this one!' She made a loud horse noise with her lips which made me laugh. She looks like a bomb has gone off in her brain. 'Right. So... I **think** I know what is going on with me but I don't know what you are going to say. Oh my God! I'm too scared to say it in case you disagree and think I'm mad!'

I encouraged her to be open and reminded her that I would never judge her. She takes another sip from her glass and I can see her hand is slightly shaking. Taking a big deep breath she quietly uttered the words, '**I think I might be autistic.**'

I had absolutely no reason **not** to believe this bright, educated woman who had just completed her final year of therapy training and can see the relief and fear in her face as she allows the words to spill out. I feel so happy for her and secretly want to shout out, Yeah, go on girl, you found your answer!! A beam stretches out across my face.

'Okay, well then! Right then! I'll be honest with you, I'm sure you're absolutely right but truthfully I don't know anything about autism. They didn't teach us anything on my course but you sound like you're pretty certain, I know you'll have done your homework, and I definitely don't think you're mad!'

That night I spent the evening learning all I could about something called 'high functioning autism' in adults so I could better support Jannine in her self-exploration and found myself unable to stop reading. As I read through Samantha Craft's females with Asperger's checklist (Craft 2012) something strange started shifting inside me. I started to download books by autistic authors and devoured 'Odd Girl Out: An Autistic Woman in a Neurotypical World' by Laura James, 'Women and Girls with Autistic Spectrum Disorder' by Sarah Hendrickx, '22 Things a Woman with Asperger's Syndrome Wants Her Partner to Know' by Rudy Simone, 'Drama Queen' by Sara Gibbs, 'Pretending to be Normal' by Liane Holliday-Willey...

For a solid week I snaffled these titles day and night and couldn't believe what I was reading. It was like my whole life was being reflected back to me. Was I autistic? Surely not, I'd have got the memo. The idea that I **might** be autistic bounced around obsessively in my head consuming my every waking thought until my next session with Stephen.

This particular Thursday I would not be all 'Helloooo!' like Mrs Doubtfire when he opens the door, instead I would feel small, stupid, embarrassed and totally convinced he would tell me I'm talking rubbish. My heart seemed to play the drum intro to 'Smells Like Teen Spirit' before I spoke and my throat began to close.

'Is everything okay today, Steph? You seem rather shaken.'

Unintentionally making the same horse noise as Jannine did, I mumbled, 'So, this **thing** kind of happened and it's sort of blown my mind. I've since done four screening questionnaires, read eight books, looked at 54 websites and I don't know how to say this but... **I think I might be autistic.**'

As the words tumbled out it was like my entire life flashed before me and I felt surrounded by all the critical grownups from my past who accused me of being too sensitive. The silence before he spoke seemed to last an eternity and I realized I was holding my breath...

All of a sudden Stephen's eyes widened and he let out a noisy 'Ah-haaa!' a bit like Alan Partridge. 'Actually, yes! That makes a lot of sense to me.' He began to chuckle to himself, nodding wildly. 'I've seen this an awful lot in my career, typically women around your age who present with supposed PTSD or complex PTSD but have actually been masking autism their whole lives. Wonderful, so what happens next and what are you going to do with this information?'

It was the strangest feeling, to be believed – to be trusted – to have someone say 'well done you, now what's your plan?' as if a path forward after a lifetime of dead ends had suddenly appeared. I tell Stephen that I'll probably look into getting a private assessment and ask him if we can pause our sessions until that's sorted. He's more than happy to speak to his boss about this and says he doubts it will be an issue. Everything feels nice and neat.

Several months later I am in my 9 o'clock assessment appointment with an amazing woman who is also autistic herself.

'Steph, I will put you out of your misery, you are so **clearly**, **obviously** autistic, but you knew that anyway.'

Her words echoed around my brain like a church bell and I felt a mix of vindication, shock and confusion. It's like the 40-odd years of assuming I was just 'a bit buggered up and weird' were washed away in an instant and replaced with clarity and peace. Everything made sense. I was autistic. I was home.

WHAT APPROACHES MIGHT WORK BEST FOR US?

So let's get down to the nitty-gritty, what is the best type of therapy for us autistics? What might make us feel worse? And do we even need therapy at all? To find out the answer to this question I devised an in-depth research questionnaire, which was completed by dozens of neurodivergent therapists and mental health workers from all corners of the globe (figure of speech, not a flat earther). I found it fascinating to read their insights not just on a professional basis but because in fact many of them:

- were late-diagnosed
- had been therapists long before they discovered they were autistic
- had gone through the same negative experiences in their own private therapy as many of us have.

As I mentioned in the disclaimer at the outset of this book the following opinions in this chapter are just that, opinions, and my advice to you is to take what you need and leave the rest. I would hate for any of the following suggestions to deter you from your own measured decision if it feels right to you.

Research tells us that the most important factor in determining a successful client outcome in therapy is the **quality of the relationship** (Elkins 2016; Martin, Garske and Davis 2000; Norcross 2002). I cannot stress enough how important this is – more important than training, time practising, techniques, modalities, concepts and qualifications. Like with everything in life, isn't it all about connection?

Interestingly the majority of our participant therapists were very open about their 'mix-and-match' eclectic style depending on client needs, which makes it kind of messy to carry out any systematic appraisal of a pure technique (damn, I love things being simple). That said, we can take some of the basic principles of each and see how and if they fit with our basic biology.

The last part of this chapter will help us decide if we might be better suited to a neurodivergent therapist – would this make life easier for us to feel understood or will our shared challenges get in the way?

So what approaches did the autistic therapists actually use? From the questionnaire, the range of therapies reported being used was wide; in alphabetical order:

- Acceptance and commitment therapy
- Animal assisted therapies
- Arts therapy
- Cognitive behavioural therapy
- Dialectical behaviour therapy
- Emotional freedom technique
- Eye movement desensitization and reprocessing
- Expressive therapies continuum
- Exposure and response prevention
- Humanistic

- Gestalt
- Integrative
- Internal family systems
- Mindfulness
- Person-centred therapy
- Play therapy
- Psychodynamics
- Psychoeducation
- Shamanic/symbolism
- Solution-focused therapy
- Transactional analysis

There isn't enough space in the book to critically appraise all the different types of approaches available (an A–Z of therapy on the British Association for Counselling and Psychotherapy website lists 33, and this doesn't take into consideration all the variations and sub-variations...) so for ease of reading I will concentrate on the ones you may be most familiar with – behavioural therapies, psychodynamic and humanistic traditions, plus a brief look into some other methods such as coaching, eye movement desensitization and reprocessing (EMDR), creative therapies and psychedelic-assisted psychotherapy.

Neurodivergent therapist James Barrott tells us:

Therapy is about supporting an individual to be able to live in a more fulfilling way – there are no prizes for sticking to a modality come what may if it is no use to the client. I do experiential exercises, psychoeducational aspects, I work outside of the therapy room, I use movement and am not always sitting down, and I recommend further reading. However, I am always in therapist mode, and everything happens within a strong therapeutic relationship and within therapeutic boundaries.

Cognitive behavioural therapy (CBT)

If you carried out a web search on the 'best therapy approaches for autism' you are extremely likely to get a range of results which won't necessarily be all that applicable to you if you have a diagnosis (or self-diagnosis) of ASD1. Presently the 'gold standard treatments' for autism include methods such as applied behaviour analysis (ABA), speech and language therapy, occupational therapy and social-relational approaches, which are used to help teach autistic people certain skills and behaviours they might struggle with.

However, if you are simply an autistic person seeking emotional support, the most **evidenced** treatment is CBT where an individual will work with a therapist – usually over a six-week period – in order to determine what the key problem is and learn to change their thinking and attitudes towards it.

One of the criticisms at the heart of CBT is that you could argue it's based on common sense and may seem victim-blaming by nature (the problem isn't the issue, the problem is your irrational thinking and cognitive distortions). In this approach it is suggested that since our thoughts, feelings and behaviours are all interlinked, changing one thing will also have a positive effect across the other areas. However, in the case of autism, it may not be possible for us to change our minds, or make sense of our feelings due to difficulties with interoception (especially with alexithymia and difficulties describing emotion), or change our behaviour without making us feel much worse.

Professor Tony Attwood explains that typical CBT may not be appropriate for us, warning how it may convince autistic people to 'tolerate the toxic'. He feels that CBT may be an appropriate treatment for accompanying low-level anxiety, anger and depression but that 'facing the fear and doing it anyway' won't make a jot of difference in convincing our nervous systems that something is okay when it isn't.

In his clinical work Tony aims to develop fundamental environmental and attitudinal changes and describes how 'any therapy which convinces us to tolerate things that are actually distressing to our mental health (be it people, situations or sensory experiences) has the potential to be hugely damaging'.

YouTuber, trainer, coach and autism advocate Paul Micallef shared with me how his work in emotional intelligence coaching has been influenced by the work of psychologist Daniel Kahneman, whose best-seller 'Thinking, Fast and Slow' considers how human beings tend to have two operating systems of thought – System One incorporating the fast, emotional and instinctive; and System Two being the slower, more considered, logical processing (sounds like autism, right?!). Paul makes the fascinating observation that the basic purpose of therapies such as CBT is to essentially develop the logical, rational brain with less reliance on feeling – something a neurotypical brain will likely need more help with, but the total opposite of our needs. He believes that engaging with this kind of approach means we will be taught 'life skills in the wrong way', learning to ignore our intuition and rely more on a thinking style already running at full capacity.

Paul's statement is really powerful, and to be honest it made me think a lot about my own life. Where was I compromising my authenticity to the 'shoulds'? It's almost like we have been conditioned to ignore our gut feelings. I know that when I don't want to do something I find it incredibly hard to just say no and leave it at that. The no whizzes around in a repetitive whirlwind full of justifications and counter-arguments as if I am on trial. But trial by whom?!

It's as if we are so traumatized from not being understood that we assume others want to challenge us and break our will. How many of us feel defensive as though our expressing a simple 'No' isn't enough? I wonder if saying no is slightly easier for some neurotypical people who may just go with their initial feeling without giving it much extra thought or detailed analysis. I see many allistic people in my practice who aren't even aware of why they do what they do (hence the need for cognitive exploration in therapies) sometimes even only able to say 'It doesn't feel right' with a shrug.

As a new rule I have started to live by this and decided to stop quantum processing my feelings. It's quite the paradigm shift, and I worry that it could lead to future error. However, now if something is causing me stress or mental anguish, it gets immediately eradicated from my life... unlike before where I felt I needed to justify my entire being just in case Saul Goodman were to pick a fight with me in a deserted Albuquerque parking lot.

Dialectical behaviour therapy (DBT)

CBT's close cousin DBT is a similar type of talk therapy which aims to help individuals manage their powerful emotions whilst simultaneously learning the art of self-acceptance. The approach, originally designed for people with borderline personality disorder, places emphasis on interpersonal relationships and psychoeducation skills, such as finding a sense of inner balance, setting boundaries, developing coping strategies (e.g. mindfulness skills) and learning how to sit in distress and overwhelm.

As with CBT this approach may be suitable for some depending on the presenting issue, but it is critical that the therapist recognizes and acknowledges our inherent social and sensory challenges and does not push us into doing something which may cause us harm. There is an emphasis on learning to describe our experiences (which may be hard...), to interact with others (which may be hard...) and experience emotions without judgement or suppression (which may be flippin' hard!) (Cunningham Abbott 2020).

The really good thing about DBT in my view is that it attempts to balance two opposing points by using the word 'and'. I have tried this myself and feel that it helps a little bit with the binary thinking nature I'm pre-disposed to, allowing me to hold two conflicting views in mind at the same time.

Acceptance and commitment therapy (ACT)

Another variation gaining popularity within modern behavioural psychology is ACT, which aims to promote cognitive flexibility. It teaches clients a range of mindfulness skills with a view to helping them surrender to things to happen (rather than avoid them) and adopt a neutral and non-judgemental connection with the environment.

Given everything we've learned in the previous chapters I don't see how this would be all that helpful as a stand-alone therapy without a big dollop of psychoeducation/coaching helping us identify what constitutes a poor environmental match for our neurotype... (I'm not going to **feel** better by convincing myself in a zen-like way that a noisy shopping centre isn't really hurting me. I do believe this is a classic masking situation, and going along with this idea will only put me at risk of a complete meltdown in Primarni).

As we've seen in my story earlier in the book, and as I've heard anecdotally from other autistic people, many therapists often tend to view avoidance as a negative coping strategy rather than as a necessary act of autistic self-preservation and healthy environmental alignment. I'm not so keen on clients being labelled as the irrational problem when neurodivergent people live in a world riddled with stigma, discrimination, stereotyping, reduced opportunities and very real barriers.

Psychoanalysis and psychodynamic therapies

The psychodynamic approach is based upon the theories of Sigmund Freud. It suggests that our early experiences determine how a person will think, behave, act and feel throughout the rest of their lives. Several of the therapists who responded to my shout-out described how they enjoy using psychodynamic therapy with their clients, feeling it can be a useful tool in helping them understand where their feelings and behaviours are coming from (as opposed to trying to change the reaction to the feeling like in CBT).

One of the key criticisms of the approach in relation to autism is, however, that it does not take into consideration biological or neurological factors which may influence our behaviour. To date there have been very few studies which look at the effectiveness of the psychodynamic approach with autistic clients (Vecchiato et al. 2016) with modern psychoanalytic theory not generally conceptualizing it either (Emanuel 2015). Professor Tony Attwood elaborates:

> These types of therapy rely upon insight and vocabulary to describe your inner feelings which is going to be very difficult with alexithymia. What I find is far more successful is art and music therapy so the person has the ability to express and explore the self through creative outlets.

Tony also shared how he once had a patient who had been in psychoanalysis and found themselves making up dreams just to satisfy the curiosity of the therapist and 'get therapy right.'

The real challenge as I see it is that, without understanding we have an autistic client sitting in front of us, our natural ways will be incorrectly assumed to be psychological disorders, ego defences and the past informing the present. As with all the approaches here it's impossible to split ourselves off and say **nothing** from our history has affected us and that it's **all** down to autism, but we would need to ensure that our therapist fully understands the complexities involved in weeding out which issues belong where.

Humanistic therapies

Humanistic therapies include approaches such as person-centred therapy, Gestalt, transactional analysis, existential therapy and solution-focused therapy.

Within person-centred therapy one of the key criticisms is that simply providing a client with empathy probably isn't enough to facilitate real change, particularly if what we are actively seeking is direction. What I value about the approach is that it leans away from the therapist being the expert, essentially placing responsibility for empowerment and self-reflection with the client. Although this approach allows the client to take the lead this may prove counter-productive if we are stuck in a rumination or only have a limited understanding of our particular situation.

Like with the other modalities discussed so far, much of the work is reliant on how a client feels (essentially drilling down to the core of the issue) so might not be suitable for those of us who struggle in this regard. Neurodivergent therapist James Barrott tells us:

The open 'feelings based' person-centred therapy done by a mediocre not very flexible therapist can almost be experienced as a punitive space where the client is getting it wrong by not knowing what to discuss or how to discuss it.

In certain circles approaches such as transactional analysis, solution-focused and existential therapy are not really thought of as systems of therapy but more about learning to see life through a particular framework. I have personally found aspects of all the above helpful in my own experience (I liked learning about relationship dynamics and contemplating my existence in the grand scheme of things). But in hindsight can't see how any of the above helped with my underlying challenges related to being autistic.

Eye movement desensitization and reprocessing (EMDR)

You might recall hearing from Dr. Naomi Fisher in the chapter on trauma, in which she describes how EMDR, which helps clients distinguish between layers of conditioning and the original trauma, can be very beneficial for autistic people in processing both simple and complex trauma.

Nobody is entirely sure (yet!) why EMDR works, but it is believed that bilateral stimulation (where a therapist will move an object left to right, use sounds over headphones, or even gentle physical stimulation such as tapping) activates and integrates both left and right hemispheres of the brain and promotes proper joined-up functioning. With the brain now communicating fully, a therapist will use guided instructions to help the client consolidate and process their particular distress, much in the same way that rapid eye movement (REM) tidies up the brain during sleep. The best way I can describe it, is that EMDR frees up trapped traumatic emotions in the brain (releasing us from a fight or flight mode stuck in the 'on' position) and helps to desensitize painful memories and reduce triggers, phobias, anxieties and fears.

One of the key strengths of the approach is that it isn't really a talk therapy as such so doesn't rely on us to label our feelings. Within a session Naomi is simply looking for an emotional arousal to work with (even if it's just feeling angry at the questions!). She believes that:

EMDR has the potential to be very accessible and I see it as creating a space for the client to do the work, like an empty structure which the client fills with their own content, compared to an approach like CBT which has more content already.

However, similar to other modalities, when used in isolation (with no additional direction, guidance, psychoeducation, homework, practical experiments, or support) we might not feel adequately resourced to make ongoing life improvements despite a reduction in our fears and anxieties.

Coaching/mentoring

In making the important distinction between therapy and coaching I spoke to autism advocate Paul Micallef who explained how coaching is more about managing the 'here and now' and not looking back at the past in order to heal. In his work if he notices that a client is struggling with PTSD triggers he may suggest psychotherapy as an option, but believes it's far less complex to manage an autistic trigger simply by changing or modifying our environment. He doesn't feel there is anything wrong with therapy in itself, offering the analogy, 'If you had a broken wrist and they gave you a wheelchair it doesn't mean there's anything wrong with the wheelchair, it's just not what was needed.'

I like Paul's analogy, which I think takes away from some of the anger we might feel if we don't seem to be improving despite our best efforts. This links back to my earlier points about how choosing the right approach and the right therapist (or coach, or mentor!) is absolutely key if we are to figure out our way forwards.

Much of Paul's work is about using his own lived experience to support the development of awareness in others, providing clear strategies and putting things into a helpful context through a variety of training resources including his YouTube channel. He cautions:

> The causes of depression and anxiety may come from completely polar opposite places on the spectrum yet present with the same symptoms. For example is it that I need to be kinder to people, or do I just need to learn to be more of an asshole? Do I need to practise gratitude more, or just accept that life can suck sometimes? The problem for us doesn't necessarily lie in experiencing the feelings (although this does become more challenging in people who also have alexithymia) but in not believing that we're allowed to run systems based on feeling.

I think it's fair to say that for many of us our moral values govern how we act in the world, often being very apologetic and not wanting to hurt other people's feelings. However, the problem with being too nice is that in compromising the self we are actually supressing our natural and healthy anger. Over time this increases our stress levels and can lead to some serious health consequences, including chronic illnesses (Dr. Gabor Maté does some amazing YouTube talks on this topic).

I probably used to be a bit of an arsehole in my punky teen days, but as I grew older, went to university, started a career and 'settled down' (shudder) I started to blend in more and behave in ways others expected. In hindsight that was the time I became more self-conscious, masked harder and internalized my anger to the point where you kind of forget you're allowed to be angry in the first place.

Whilst I am not advocating you decide to be an arsehole (although if you want to reduce your number of fucks given I will support you fully), I do think it's important for us to tap into that healthy inner drive which is there to keep us safe. Caring too much about others' feelings can leave us in a really vulnerable position as we feel guilty for putting boundaries in place.

My own inner anger was spontaneously awoken a few summers ago when a driver who wasn't paying attention to the road nearly ran me over. He had the audacity to yell at **me** through the window. Despite spending the last 20 years calm and avoiding conflict at all costs, I found myself unexpectedly running after the car hurling abuse and probably looking a bit like Leatherface in the last scene of 'The Texas Chainsaw Massacre'. I came home feeling very proud of myself. But are there other less dramatic ways of connecting and expressing angry feelings in a safer environment?

Creative therapies

There's a growing body of evidence to suggest that creative arts and expressive therapies (things like music, art, dance, acting, even comedy) might be beneficial to autistic people, allowing us to access feelings without questioning the legitimacy of them (no, Saul Goodman, not today!) and without needing to process them via thoughts in a way which might prove really difficult.

Professor Tony Attwood explains how if he is working with a depressed client who is struggling to articulate the depth of their pain he might suggest they go away and compile a playlist which reflects their inner landscape, or find a scene from a film, or a part in a Harry Potter book. 'They say a picture is worth a thousand words – could you find 20 images on Google that represents your torment?' He also reflects on how many autistic people naturally gravitate towards the arts because it is a space of self-expression and self-exploration stating that, 'If we are going to use therapy in its broadest sense we need to start looking at arts and music.'

Neurodivergent art therapist Louise Weston agrees sharing:

I feel that art therapy itself is often seen as unconventional yet still works within evidence-based frameworks. I personally use whichever methods are suited to best cater to my client relationally and take it at their pace. Oftentimes my clients have tried other modalities and find different results through art making. Or they are seeking to balance out other therapies and use the materials to help regulate, release, restore, reframe, repair, or reset – often with very little said – yet still communicated.

I call upon breathing, movement, sights, sounds and smells to complement my practice as well. Working somatically gives an opportunity to teach my clients to become attuned to their needs through signals in their bodies and recognize triggers or warning signs, prior to reaching the point of meltdown.

Psychedelic-assisted therapy

I recently attended a presentation on the use of psilocybin (the compound found in certain mind-altering fungi) in treating non-treatable depression. The speaker (Dr. Chris Timmerman – a neuroscientist and a leading researcher in a neuropsychopharmacology study at Imperial College London) explained how depressed brains usually fall into a rigid thinking pattern which they cannot get out of (think of it as stuck on a loop). His research demonstrated that such psychedelic tools can encourage more neural connectivity and boot us off the 'default mode network' negative loops.

Whilst a neuroscientific exploration of trauma is beyond the scope of this book the important thing is that we can start to understand that trauma isn't just an event or series of events that **happens** to us, it is a recalibration of our internal systems and perceptions (including changes within the limbic system and even gene expression).

The Multidisciplinary Association for Psychedelic Studies[1] is an American not-for-profit organization which seeks to raise awareness and understanding of psychedelic substances. Their website is filled with promising research exploring how substances like magic mushrooms, LSD, MDMA and cannabis (including CBD products) can help autistic people with challenges such as social anxiety and finding greater cognitive flexibility. There are also a great deal of exciting developments around other compounds such as ayahuasca, ketamine and ibogaine, and I'm grateful to be living in a time where governments are slowly coming around to the idea that these

---

1   https://maps.org

plants and chemicals have incredibly useful applications in the world of healing. Is the mind–body connection finally catching on?

Alternative approaches

In my research I also came across countless other therapies which profess to help autistic individuals have a reduction in 'symptoms' (e.g. somatic experiencing, Reiki, transcranial magnetic stimulation, acupuncture, neurofeedback…). Yet many of these approaches lack any kind of rigorous scientific evidence to substantiate their claims. I'm as open-minded as the next person but I don't think it would be of much benefit (and probably a bit irresponsible too) to start suggesting methods which may only help some individuals some of the time. I'm actually a massive fan of Reiki and hold my first two degrees in it, but can I honestly say it works for everyone?

Final thoughts on therapies

To me it really comes down to three variables – the unique client, the therapist's toolkit, and the connection. You could even argue that with a well-enough attuned therapist you could make anything the basis of a therapy. I actually see no harm in a client using their special interest as a focus if that would help them maximize their experience – in fact it could be a great starting point if that's what the client felt comfortable with as a way into the therapy.

I would describe myself as both humanistic and pluralistic (the latter meaning that you create a bespoke therapy for your client). I'm certainly not averse to art, music, nature, movement, breathwork, meditation, screaming into cushions, animals, memes, photos, quotes, acting or psychedelic-based add-ons.

I believe that as knowledge-craving creatures, with a desire to know why things are as they are, that any therapy without an element of psychoeducation[2] might not be all that good for us (essentially guessing what's happening without it being made explicit and therefore highly confusing). I also see the incredible value of a joint coaching and therapy approach. I don't feel we do our clients any favours by always letting them work it out for themselves, which in many cases can feel torturous.

Single session therapy (SST) – where a client just has a one-off session – may also prove valuable for us as it offers help at the point of need. But it doesn't seem to be all that popular, well-known or even available! Personally I have about eight different moods a day and what will be bothering me on a Tuesday might not need a follow-up visit the following counselling week (much to the therapist's disappointment and love of continuity!).

It's important to note that with any of the therapies listed here, that there are also many satisfied autistic customers who have found the approaches really beneficial to their personal growth. I guess it all really does depend on what you're trying to work on.

CASE STUDY: MICHAEL

The following case study has been contributed by 42-year-old Michael. That is not his real name but he is a very real and lovely person. My thanks go to him for sharing his experience.

'I was drawn to psychodynamic therapy at the age of 38. Not, as I

---

2   Psychoeducation involves learning about your mental health – a practitioner may give you information in person or through a handout explaining about a particular topic. For example, 'What physiological changes occur if I'm having a panic attack?' The idea being that the more we know, the better equipped we are to manage our difficult experiences. We may then conclude, 'I'm not actually having a heart attack, it's just stress hormones making my chest feel tight.'

understand is commonplace, because I had reached a difficult or transitional stage in my life, but because I had found myself at a markedly happy moment – I had decided to move by myself to Barcelona after 15 years in London. I was living alone, was happily single, and was thriving professionally. In my newly contented state, and with the introspection all of that offered, I wanted to explore some long-held curiosities about myself: Why am I such a 'late bloomer' in so many ways, outside of my professional life? Why do I derive so much joy from time spent alone, especially living alone? And, most importantly, why do I find romantic relationships so difficult to navigate?

'My assumption was that exploring each of these questions in the psychodynamic environment would reveal obscured truths and traumas in my past that once aired and deconstructed, would allow me to move forward and become more whole, that is, more "normal". I felt a great deal of shame around my perceived shortcomings, and being a ravenous consumer of books and podcasts on psychotherapy, I was excited to begin what I assumed was indisputably positive work.'

'What followed was an extremely painful period. Emboldened by my newfound commitment to weekly therapy sessions, I attempted to move away from my "natural programming" and pursue the trappings of the life I thought I should be living. I made several major life decisions which went against my natural instincts – I recall the pain in pressing forward with a house purchase to which the instinctive part of me howled in protest. I sat in therapy each week, often anxious and emotional, in growing mistrust of my gut feelings, which I assumed were the restrictive voices of past trauma holding me back from my goal of being whole.'

'My attempt to carve out a "normal" life for myself led me into a very dark place, and an emotional nadir. I was in a relationship that I did not find fulfilling and had embarked on a property renovation project with which I could not cope – later I would realize I had far exceeded the limits of my executive function – a state of high stress which lasted for a year, compounded by the chaos and fear of the Covid-19 pandemic.'

'At the lowest moment of that year I stumbled across an article about a prominent actor who had 'come out' as autistic, discussing how he lived a fairly isolated and restricted life out of choice, musing on the joy that gave him. Curious, I researched the other signs of autism, and my heart started to race as I recognized myself, my habits and my outlook on life reflected back at me. I booked an assessment and within two months had received a positive diagnosis.'

'The weeks after the diagnosis were an emotional rollercoaster – I felt tremendously sad to have discovered this so late in life, and thought of how I might have better managed my life, and treated those around me, had I known from a young age. At the same time, I felt incredible joy that I could finally live life on my own terms, without feeling somehow 'less' or 'not enough'. I pledged I would no longer listen to the "shoulds".'

CHOOSING THE RIGHT THERAPIST – NEURODIVERGENT OR NEUROTYPICAL?

'In my art therapy group Zoom last week, it came up that autistic therapists are also a priority for me. With the double empathy problem and needing empathy for a therapeutic relationship, it just makes more sense to me. Someone whose mind operates more like mine. Otherwise it feels like someone's trying to fix a Mac with PC software, a frustrating experience for everyone.'

Pros and cons of neurodivergent therapists

From the neurodivergent therapists I interviewed the majority of them expressed that being neurodivergent gave them a range of skills and cognitive abilities which are incredibly helpful in the counselling room. Many described how their love of learning and psychology as a special interest made continuing professional development easy. They shared how they excelled in areas such as:

- hyper-empathy
- pattern recognition (connecting the dots and solving puzzles)
- being blunt, direct and honest
- not entering into power games with clients
- hyper-focus (showing full attention)
- attention to detail
- exceptional memories supporting a huge synthesis of data (as if mentally recording each session and calling up archives wherever required)
- deep intuition
- taking things literally (trusting the client's words and being curious rather than judging and assuming)
- ultimately identifying with the neurodivergent perspective from an experiential position.

UK-based therapist Kat Healey explains how she finds it easy to spot a neurodivergent client, 'Something internal sparks in me, I think I have a radar fitted, and a kind of "autocue" running in my head when people speak where my brain highlights more words/patterns when I hear someone with autism!'

The therapists also described some of the downsides of being a neurodivergent therapist. These included the potential of burnout sometimes making them unreliable, although it's worth noting that compassion fatigue is something which affects workers in all the caring professions and is not exclusive to autistic professionals. They also shared challenges such as:

- misunderstanding elements of conversation (e.g. taking sarcasm literally)
- experiencing sensory disturbances in sessions themselves (this was typically more when therapists were using facilities and offices that were not their own)
- difficulties with interpreting client communication relating to flat affect and/or hyper-or hypo-facial expressions (also trying to manage their own faces!).

Licensed Professional Counselor Christin Fontes adds:

> Of course, I'm tracking with my clients. I am deeply invested; I am listening, and I care... a lot. But that is not always clear by looking at my face. Even when my face is making the appropriate facial expressions, the movement in the corners of my mouth and eyes are quick and return to neutral. What I call neutral others may read as annoyance or lack of interest.

There is of course the concern of over-identification perhaps due to our rigid thinking patterns ('this is how I experience autism so you probably see things as I do'). In my own work I have to be careful about making assumptions and make sure I am asking the right questions in order to stay within the client's frame of reference, and wearing two radars – the autistic one and the trauma one – where is the disturbance coming from and how do they intersect? Neurodivergent therapist Claire Ratcliffe shared her experience of this first hand,

Several years ago, I had sessions with an autistic therapist. However, I found I wasn't being seen as an individual. The therapist would say things such as 'Well, you're autistic so of course you like...' and would go on to say something that wasn't true for me. Therefore I often felt missed, and that assumptions were being made about me that were incorrect and were more about the therapist's own experiences.

Can neurotypical therapists be just as effective?

Although not identifying as autistic himself, Professor Tony Attwood describes himself as a sort of 'NT/ND bilingual and hybrid', with autism being present in his immediate family allowing him to bridge the communication divide from a place of intuition. From his position, he recognizes that neither culture is superior, only different, and that we should all avoid the trappings of judgement.

In my personal life I have friends who are both neurodivergent and neurotypical and I don't think it would serve me well to only identify with one type of person. I would caution opting for an autistic therapist simply because they share your neurotype if actually you don't really resonate with them, you don't feel they get you or they lack training and qualifications. Therapist Mairead Keogan shared how,

When I was starting to question 'maybe I really am autistic', I didn't have as much knowledge of autism and there was a lot of self-doubt because I didn't fit the stereotypical presentation of autism shown in media. The therapist I saw at the time didn't have any training/speciality in autism but I still brought it up with her. Despite not having the knowledge she still validated me and allowed me to begin exploring that. I went on to work with a therapist who did have training in autism and that helped me finally accept my autism, but that first therapist's validation and holding space for me really opened the door.

I think the story goes to show that even if you don't have a lot of knowledge around neurodivergence you can start to show up for your clients by looking up some basic information and be that initial support for them.

Autism advocate Paul Micallef also recommends looking around for what will help you get the right answers, warning that a therapist advertising as an 'autism specialist' doesn't necessarily mean they will be the most skilled. This can be particularly true if the training is outdated and/or excludes autistic voices. 'In my experience,' he says, 'it can be easier to educate a therapist rather than re-educate them.'

Top 10 therapist suggestions on choosing a therapist

- Make sure you feel comfortable with your therapist.
- Don't judge a book by its cover – connection and safety develop over time and you won't be able to immediately get that information from somebody's online profile.
- Set yourself an end goal – what will completed therapy look like for you? How will you know when you are feeling better?
- Be wary. Does it feel like your therapist is simply happy to take your money every week or do you feel like you are getting somewhere slowly?

- Ask around – who comes on good recommendation? Are those sources reliable? Real? Are they autistic?
- Do you feel safe, understood, heard and respected?
- Is your therapist flexible and can accommodate you, or do you feel they are expecting you to conform to their own methodology and frameworks?
- Are they informed on neurodiversity? And if so, what does that mean – an online certificate, a one-day course, training delivered by autistic people?
- Do they have lived experience of autism (either personally or within their close connections)?
- Are you picking up on any signs of ableism (made explicitly or implicitly)?

With respect to the last two points, remember it's okay to ask these questions – this is about your decision and what works best for you. Christin Fontes suggests:

> In an initial session ask them outright what they know about autism, their experiences working with clients with autism, and their perspective on autistic adults. You'd be surprised how many practising clinicians knowingly or unknowingly hold harmful viewpoints. It isn't your job to educate them, but it is your job to steer clear of them.

I wish I'd known all this stuff when I embarked on my own therapy journey all those years ago. Looking back I knew absolutely nothing and probably thought you just went to therapy, said some stuff, they told you the answers and boom, you were fixed. I remember being obsessed with therapist qualifications and their training – would they know enough, who was the most qualified, who was the best? What if they didn't know the thing I needed to know?

That line of thinking, which to be fair would work really well if we were talking about heart surgery or having your root canal fixed, just doesn't apply to (as Tony Attwood says) the 'art' of therapy. The relationship is everything.

So now as we approach the end of the book, can we unequivocally state that neurotypical therapy **really** works for neurodivergent brains? Do we even need therapy in the first place? Or do we just need to create a neurodivergent-friendly life which alleviates our stress and anxiety? It's a real head-scratcher, but I'll hand you over to the neurodivergent therapists and the autistic community to judge that for yourself.

SUMMARY

- While some of the more well-known therapeutic methods, including cognitive behavioural therapy, psychodynamic and humanistic traditions, may offer some help, they have downsides for neurodivergent clients.
- Interventions such as coaching, eye movement desensitization and reprocessing (EMDR), creative therapies and psychedelic-assisted psychotherapy may better support us.
- Making decisions from feeling rather than from intelligence and logic can be difficult for us, but thinking from our gut may be a skill we develop over time.
- There are both benefits and challenges in choosing a neurodivergent therapist.
- Top 10 professional suggestions to help you choose the best practitioner for your needs.

Chapter 8

SO DOES NEUROTYPICAL THERAPY WORK FOR NEURODIVERGENT BRAINS?

WHAT NEURODIVERGENT THERAPISTS THINK

When I started writing this book, given my own positive experiences in therapy (albeit few and far between I think you'll have gathered by now!) and seeing the benefit it can bring to others' lives too, I assumed that all the participant data and expert opinions would come back as 'Yaaas therapy is a great option for autistic humans!!' Only that's not how things have panned out at all. We've taken a look at some of the evidence and rationale for why it might not be all that effective, or better said, not all that effective delivered in the way it so often is.

Here's what some of the neurodivergent therapists and coaches had to say in response to the question posed in the chapter title.

In my experience, no. The ASD clients I work with are more interested in conversational approach. Most neurotypical clinicians like to be a wall, and I have previous employers who got mad when I was transparent with clients. – Michelle Hunt

They do, but not to the extent that they may work for neurotypical people. – James Barrott

It only works on a very basic level. For example CBT brings awareness of some tools like the Worry Tree, or the Unhelpful Thinking Styles, that increases emotional literacy. Perhaps CBT can be helpful to treat a specific area or issue. – Mariano Hvozda

We have tried many in our family before I found a neurodivergent therapist, which has been the most successful and life-changing to be honest. I think it's down to the person providing the service though and their understanding of neurodivergence. I know that my clients have expressed that my lived experience of having a neurodivergent family has benefited their therapeutic experience as well as helping their parents or carers gain greater insights about their children. – Louise Weston

Based on the fact that talk therapy has been rewarding in my own case, I do think it can definitely be appropriate. It is, as in most cases, about the relationship between patient and therapist, and that the latter has an interest in understanding the patient's perspective – and a certain sensitivity to the fact that a neurodivergent individual might have a slightly different way of experiencing, processing and understanding themselves both intrapsychically and relationally. – Jonas Dunér

Yes and no. No – I think many traditional neurotypical talk therapies are based on ableist, colonialist, Euro-centric ideas that don't work for a lot of people. They are based on the idea that there is a correct way to be, correct way to act, correct way to think, and if one isn't being/acting/thinking that way they must change. Yes – if the therapy is focused on helping the person understand themself, trust themself, know themself, and love themself even when they don't conform to cultural expectations, then they can work with neurodivergent brains. I do think there is a limit to any therapy if someone doesn't know they are neurodivergent and is trying to measure themselves to a neurotypical yardstick. – Jennifer Glacel

Specific techniques from certain modalities can work for some neurodivergent people, but it is a spectrum and what works for one person may not work for another depending on their needs. – Mairead Keogan

The chances of a neurotypical talk therapist knowing enough about the neurodivergent experience to tailor their therapy to help the neurodivergent client is slim to none. I had to get extremely lucky. Traditional talk therapy 'worked' for me on a situational level. I had a problem with a co-worker, so we worked on navigating that issue. There was conflict within my family, so we worked on strategies to make it out of that conflict without damaging the relationship. However, when I zoom out, it didn't give me the skills to understand my experiences so that I could take those skills and apply them generally across different domains of my life.

Traditional talk therapy worked until my therapists (plural because it happened with more than one) thought that I was just grasping at straws to find reasons to stay in treatment, looking for reasons to not grow. I became the problem. More directly, my undiagnosed autism became the problem. And for it, I was harmed at the hands of multiple therapists. Even though it was their job to pick up on it, it was their job to help me, but they didn't. I was never given the tools to make life a little easier. I carried trauma from my real life into the therapist's offices and walked out with new trauma. In short, I think traditional neurotypical talk therapies can work, but the stars have to align in such a way for that to be true – and far too often, they don't. – Christin Fontes

To be honest, I think it comes down to the professional sensibility to understand the neurodivergent client's needs. All approaches can do harm or help, and their execution may vary greatly depending on the professional. – Luis Reis

No. And my experience of 1000+ people would largely agree with this. Traditional therapies appear to have a neurotypical focus and attempt to achieve a goal of returning a person to 'normal' functioning – sociability, variety, etc. This is clearly flawed for neurodivergent people and can leave them feeling that they are not only failing at life, but failing at therapy too because they are 'not trying hard enough'. Approaches which focus on the past as a reason for behaviours/thoughts can be misleading, and in my experience autistic people appear to want practical strategies for managing challenges rather than knowing whose fault it was for them.

I have had numerous therapists prior to and after diagnosis and all but one have been awful. I have felt worse after seeing them. A hypnotherapist recently told me that he wished he had my problems, because I only worked part-time and he had to keep two jobs – I went for panic attacks which made me agoraphobic for several years... losing my career as a speaker and trainer. I went to a CBT therapist and disclosed being autistic. I then spent two sessions (which I paid for) teaching him about autism and how he needed to work with me. He seemed completely out of his depth and knew less than I did, so I gave up.

The only positive experience that I have had was many years ago before I knew anything about being autistic. I was in a very bad place and she was just extremely wise and gentle. A bit too vague and spiritual for me, but I went along with it because she was so accepting of me. She knew nothing about autism, but I guess I just got lucky. – Sarah Hendrickx

WHAT DO I THINK?

When I think about how I have always approached therapy with clients (way before I knew I was autistic) I can see that I've always just treated others in the way I'd want to be treated. I don't really have an agenda in a session. I listen out for what it is a client might need, and I do not assume they know what course of action to take. I know from experience if I say I don't know something, it's because I really don't bloody know something. I'm not being difficult, avoidant or evasive, I just don't know.

I have seen that being the type of dogmatic-refusing-to-budge-arrogant-practitioner can cause immense pain and suffering to others, and that we find ourselves on the receiving end of mind games, ego and power trips we simply aren't even competing in. I believe that for autistic people therapy shouldn't be about **adapting a technique**, but instead having the practitioner learn to set aside their preconceived ideas, try and imagine what our worlds look like, and help us to celebrate the neurodivergent perspective. I've had many clients come to me saying how devastated they are to discover they're autistic, only to dig away and unearth that they're seeing autism through the eyes of stigma and ableism.

The big question I think we all need to ask ourselves before we go to therapy is **What is it I am trying to fix or cure?** Are the mental health challenges I face just by-products of living out of kilter with my environment (e.g. I'm gluten intolerant and will have a whole host of nasty side effects if I have a slice of pizza – but does that make me 'ill'?). And put simply, what's causing your 'symptoms'?

For me our key task in therapy, coaching or whatever approach feels right is to go back to basics and create a neurodivergent-friendly life which works for **us**. But does an autistic person **need** psychological therapy **because** they're autistic? Absolutely not. There is nothing wrong with you. You might need to do some work to adjust your own negative perceptions of yourself after a lifetime of feeling mad, bad and defective, but trust me, you're ace.

In my years of experience I have come to recognize that often the person sitting in the chair isn't really the one who should be sitting there at all. Arseholes will always be arseholes. It's your job to recognize they're arseholes and stay the funk away. I think neuro-affirming therapy allows us to normalize our experience and give ourselves the permission we need to shine our true colours. Other people don't like it? Take that as information and move on. What is it you want your life to look like? That bright pink hat with blue furry shoes? Do it! Quitting your ludicrously highly paid job in finance to run a second-hand bookshop specializing in Hello Kitty? Hell to the yes!

Anything other than following the path with heart will inevitably lead us down the path of mental anguish. I have learned this the hard way. I spent the first three and a half decades of my life contorting myself to fit with what I thought society wanted from me. At one stage I worked 60 hours a week, endlessly climbing the greasy pole of success, and what did I find was at the top of it? A big pile of nothingness. I realize now that actually I'm not governed by money or notoriety, and if I'm being perfectly honest the dream outcome for writing this book is that it will help people avoid the trauma I've gone through and then I can be left alone to enjoy the peace and quiet of my garden.

And on that horticultural theme – some plants will thrive in bright sunshine, others will wilt and die – convincing a peace lily to just pull themselves together seems a bit much in my humble opinion.

All too often clients feel powerless to write their own experiential narratives of the therapy process itself – because the therapist knows best, right? Their educated guesses and clinical assumptions are backed up with credentials and certificates after all. I am reminded that therapy isn't something that is done **to us**, it should be done **with us**, or better said – the client knows where the pain lies and should be trusted. I personally believe that therapy is absolutely brilliant when done correctly (so won't be giving up the day job just yet!). And it never fails to amaze me how powerful the human spirit is in its capacity to heal.

OTHER NON-THERAPY OPTIONS

The truth is not everyone can afford to go to therapy but that doesn't have to be the end of the conversation. Remember, therapy is only fairly recent in the grand scheme of history and squillions of people have lived before, learned to self-regulate and overcome their personal challenges. When I was putting this book together I was very mindful that therapy might not be the best answer for everyone so did a shout out on my Instagram page to see how you prefer to work on yourselves. Here's what you shared:

- Meditation
- Journaling
- Punching my bed hard (boxing) or screaming into a pillow to release tension
- A really tight hug from my partner
- Dancing
- Singing (especially loud diaphragmatic singing which increases heart rate variability and oxytocin, and activates both the sympathetic nervous system and vagus nerve)
- Alternate nostril breathing
- The Wim Hof method
- EFT tapping
- Yoga

- Tai chi or qigong
- Martial arts
- Spending time with animals
- Stimming
- A very cold shower (personally this would kill me with my skin sensitivities but there we go!)
- Cardio exercises (but can make some people feel much worse due to adrenaline spikes and feeling overwhelmed by overheating)
- Affirmations
- Laughter
- Prayer
- Massage/reflexology
- Reiki
- Taking supplements such as zinc, omega-3 fatty acids EPA and DHA, pre-/probiotics
- Acupuncture
- Being in nature (lots of people said this was very helpful for them)
- Art
- Progressive muscle relaxation
- Watching something familiar like 'Friends' (Could I *be* any more in agreement?!)
- Medication (though not for everybody)

I personally find that there is no shame in using medications such as antidepressants if you find that supports you to cope. My only concern is that these kinds of psychotropic substances do not cure mental health issues but act as a kind of relief, and it's safe to say that the myth of 'chemical imbalance' has long been debunked. I do feel it's important that we learn to sit with some degree of distress (to the best of our abilities and capacity), as emotion-numbing medication may counter-productively deny us the opportunity to develop resilience, and therefore could inhibit personal growth.

Again it's important to consider what we need help with – a co-morbid anxiety or depression which might be better supported by lifestyle and environmental changes, or helping the body to calm itself when it simply struggles of its own accord.

SUGGESTIONS FOR GOOD PRACTICE FROM THE EXPERTS – YOU!

I believe that any clinical practice, intervention or support service should be designed and driven **by** neurodivergent people – not as a tokenistic engagement but as absolutely crucial to delivering effective approaches which work.

Here's what you told me you wanted from therapy:

- To be believed and supported to communicate your needs.
- Help with managing uncertainty.
- Things being spelled out at times.
- The use of metaphors and analogies around special interests.
- Social skills support (practical things).
- Help to change environments (accessibility/reduced demands/creating a life which nourishes, not drains).
- Radical acceptance, not being required to conform with a neurotypical life which is too much for us.
- A focus on strengths.
- Being treated with respect and equality.
- Having access barriers removed (such as not having to use the phone to make appointments, filling in lots of paperwork, homework assignments, having to stay for the full session, or attending sessions every week if not feeling that is manageable – offering flexibility).
- Assertiveness training.

- Support when figuring out the specifics of what to say to someone (e.g. role playing a conflict, writing out preparation scripts for interviews/dates).
- Self-advocacy (and being able to fight for us if necessary) – providing actual support when external individuals and agencies are not accommodating our differences.
- A different approach – alternatives to traditional routes working **with** the autistic brain (not against it).
- Each autistic person to be treated as a unique individual.
- Curiosity exercised when a client can't/won't do what's expected or needed.
- Seeing barriers as an external problem to be addressed together.
- Exits allowed for without pressure to explain.
- Regulation and co-regulation skills.
- Acknowledgement of the pain of living in and navigating a hostile and unpredictable world not made for us.
- Compassion.
- Explanations of what counselling is, what is required from us and how it works (clear and accessible, using information sheets).
- Boundaries and limits set without blame/shame.
- Behaviours seen as communication and no assumptions made.
- Real understanding of autism, not just from the medical model perspective, but from learning about our neurodivergent experience from the autistic community/ social model of disability.

A 2019 study (Camm-Crosbie et al.) carried out a thematic research project which explored the views of 200 autistic people and their experiences of mental health treatment and support. They found that their participants expressed a need for individually tailored treatments and support, identifying a number of key themes including:

- Difficulties in accessing treatment and support.
- A general lack of clinical knowledge about autistic people with co-occurring mental health issues.
- A lack of appropriate support being linked to a decline in wellbeing and suicide being considered as an option.

Given the name of the project alone ('People Like Us Don't Get Support') I would argue that there is still a shed load of work to do to ensure neurodivergent voices are being truly involved in service design and delivery. None of the above suggestions are that difficult to accommodate for the majority of practitioners out there, and there is nothing wrong (repeat, **nothing wrong!**) with asking your therapist to make adjustments so you can get the most out of your sessions. If they seem hesitant, unwilling, or even just a bit put out – take that as information and look elsewhere.

You're not being difficult in asserting your autistic needs, you're doing a cracking job of self-advocacy.

SUGGESTED ACCOMMODATIONS FROM THE THERAPISTS

I allow my clients to contact me whenever. Clients knowing they can text my work phone, or send an email or voice note has increased safety and allowed for more information sharing and trust. For other accommodations, I purchased an auto email-sending application that sends email reminders to clients to accommodate for executive dysfunction. I help with filling out paperwork (or ask a colleague if they can), help with planning out interpersonal interactions, and overall just assessing needs and doing everything I can within the

confines of my abilities to help set the client up for success.
– Michelle Hunt

I am aware of sensory needs and change lighting, sound, etc. as needed. I have a variety of fidgets and other sensory items (weighted blanket, for example) for use as needed. – Jennifer Glacel

I've made changes to formats of homework assignments (e.g. recording a voice memo instead of answering a prompt because it did not work for a client) and incorporate special interests (music, video games, etc.) into their sessions. If we're doing a virtual session and they're having a rough day I allow them to turn the camera off or use the chat feature if they cannot verbally speak. – Mairead Keogan

I often use breathing exercises and assist a client to notice any effects in their body as we speak. I bring into a session such things as checking how they are with the temperature in the room, if they are thirsty, if the chair is comfortable. We can experiment – for instance use cushions, or get them to try different chairs to see if one feels more supportive, being patient and giving them time to organize the space. – James Barrott

I have always tried to think about how that specific individual would best take on this information/concept and adapt the delivery method accordingly. This may mean sketches, spreadsheets, graphs, etc. Logic and proof are usually essential for neurodivergent clients when considering changes to their thoughts or behaviours. – Sarah Hendrickx

AND IN CONCLUSION...

After the first twelve months of post-diagnosis shock had subsided and I began to experience life as if for the first time, I started to feel somewhat invincible as if I had cracked some kind of code. Everything started making complete sense and in the process of rewriting my history, my entire personality went through a systems update too.

Almost everything in my world has changed in recent times – the focus of my work, the realistic number of hours I can manage without burning out, the type of relationships I will allow (I said goodbye to a significant amount of people who I could no longer relate to), my appearance, and even what I choose to eat on a daily basis (so what if I like chicken and rice every day, it's not a crime, is it?!). It hurt to make many of those changes and really did feel like letting go of a past life, but the reality is it was killing me. I'm no longer running on the neurotypical hamster-wheel.

These days I still feel like I'm on the outside looking in but am quite content to sit on the front row with a bag of popcorn and a big slurpy drink, because I now know that I'm not alone – there are millions of other people **like me** who get it, and that brings me a huge sense of comfort. We are not failed neurotypicals, we are bloody amazing autistic people with incredible cognitive strengths and abilities who deserve to be treated as equals, not lesser human beings. We need validation, vindication, guidance, opportunities and empathy, not sympathy and cures.

Only you will be able to decide what is causing pain in your own life but I'll bet that when you start to take a serious inventory your body is communicating what's okay and what's not loud and clear. Whether your challenges stem from existing in a mismatched environment, an accumulation of upsetting experiences or simply part of your basic biology, it's worth remembering that we are all capable of improving our lives and situations. Will I ever be free from anxiety? I doubt it! The unknown men knocking on my front door tonight (despite the 'No salesmen' sticker on the letterbox!) made me and the cat leap about 12 feet in the air, but do I feel better equipped to manage whatever life throws at me after investing in my mental health journey? Definitely.

Learning to say no and setting boundaries can be extremely difficult for those of us who have shape-shifted ourselves beyond recognition to please others and fit in. But the truth is, now you know what you need to do (prioritizing your needs and creating a neurodivergent-friendly life), it is vital you undertake that challenge and start taking up the space you deserve. I can't help but feel that our inner compass has been calling out to us all along, but its tiny voice has been buried under the years of conditioning instructing us to ignore our wishes and be someone we're not.

In my opinion the only thing that should need 'fixing' in therapy is the damage done to our self-esteem. If you haven't already given it yourself, I grant you full permission to go out and live **your** life in whatever way feels good.

I sincerely hope that this book has given you some food for thought, a few tools to help you on your journey, some tips to avoid potential harm (a map) and feel just that little bit more confident to ask the right kinds of questions. There are countless therapists out there who work nothing short of magic with clients and I hope you are able to find the right match for you. There has never been a better time in history to be alive when it comes to neurodiversity, and I know that things will only get better the more our voices are heard. So go on out there, make waves (or wave dem bloomers!) and don't settle for anything less than you deserve. You've got this. I see you.

With much love,

Steph xo

SUMMARY

- Most neurodivergent professionals have reservations about whether traditional therapy can work for autistic people in a fully effective way.
- The key task in therapy is to create a neurodivergent-friendly life which works for us.
- There are numerous alternative non-therapy options (mostly free) used by the autistic community.
- Therapists can make specific accommodations and adaptations, which you might like to ask for.
- There are many good therapists out there, and the world is getting better for neurodivergents – we just have to make sure our voices are heard.

Notes from Tony Attwood

We need an autistic consumer's perspective of therapy. The experiences and themes described by Steph Jones will be invaluable for both therapists and autistic adults and their families. Her survival guide will also facilitate the development of new therapy models specifically designed for the autistic way of perceiving, thinking, learning and relating.

The different perceptions associated with autism can include extreme sensitivity to external sensory experiences (exteroception), and sometimes difficulty perceiving internal body sensations such as heart rate, breathing and muscle tension (interoception). These signals are important in perceiving increasing distress and agitation.

Thinking can be different in terms of 'thinking in pictures' as described by Temple Grandin and a tendency for cognitive rigidity, or 'one track mind' especially when anxious or stressed. The different ways of learning can be a preference for learning in solitude, the tendency to focus on details and an idiosyncratic approach to problem-solving. Relating can differ regarding the ability to read non-verbal communication and social context, making and keeping friends and experiencing rejection and bullying at school and work.

All of these differences may contribute to the sorts of issues in the therapeutic relationship that Steph highlights so insightfully in her book.

There are specific diagnostic criteria for autism, but it is rare for an autistic adult to only be autistic; that is to have 'autism pure'. It is most likely that the person may have autism plus, that is plus, high levels of anxiety, ADHD, depression, eating or personality disorder, and signs of trauma.

There is also the issue of the person's adaptation to autism in that they may be socially isolated due to personal preference (extreme introversion), feel safer alone, or have comorbid mental health issues; or engaging socially by camouflaging and suppressing autistic characteristics and their true selves.

The autistic adult may create (unconsciously or consciously) a social persona, contributing to mental exhaustion, depression, and a lack of authenticity. No wonder autistic individuals often seek therapy, but does the therapist understand autism and the life experiences and expectations of an autistic client?

A therapist may have had limited training and previous and ongoing supervision in the adaptations to therapy to accommodate an autistic client's different way of perceiving, thinking, learning and relating. As Steph Jones points out in this incredibly useful book, they may not be familiar with developing conceptualizations and theoretical models of autism, such as Theory of Mind, double empathy, camouflaging, autistic burnout, and being the authentic self. There may be the anticipation that conventional therapy will automatically be successful, but conventional therapy is based on the conventional, not the autistic mind.

The sensory aspects of the therapy room must be reviewed and modified according to an autistic client's sensory profile. This can include auditory experiences such as the sound of electric and electronic equipment, lighting systems such as fluorescent lighting and bright sunlight, aromas such as perfumes, deodorants and cleaning products and tactile experiences such as seating fabrics.

There is another sensory sensitivity that needs to be considered, which is an autistic client possibly being extraordinarily perceptive and reactive to any negative thoughts and feelings of a therapist or fellow clients in a group or residential setting. This is autistic emotional empathy. Clinical experience, autobiographies and social media describe a 'sixth sense' ability to perceive someone's 'negativity', which can 'infect' and dominate the mood of an autistic client. Social withdrawal is not always because of being socially confused; it can be a protection mechanism to avoid being contaminated by someone's negative feelings.

The differences in thinking can include alexithymia, an important issue in therapy. Alexithymia is a diminished vocabulary to describe different levels of emotional experience, especially subtle and complex emotions. Alexithymia is not exclusive to autism, but most (60% of) autistic clients have difficulty explaining their reasoning and emotional state using conversational speech. There may also be reduced internal emotion recognition (interoception), and their narrative may focus on external rather than internal experience. There may be an accurate description of the sequence of events and actions, but limited reference to someone's or their own thoughts and feelings.

Within therapy, alexithymia can lead to difficulty answering the question, 'How do you feel about that?' or 'Why did you do that?' The autistic client is not evasive or obtuse but may have genuine difficulty answering the question due to alexithymia. However, creative therapies such as art, music and drama therapy, and journaling and typing rather than talking can be used to facilitate self-expression and self-exploration and incorporated into therapy to accommodate alexithymia.

Other autistic thinking characteristics may include difficulty coping with change and rigid thinking patterns, which are included in the DSM5-TR diagnostic criteria for autism spectrum disorder. Thus, there may be some resistance to the therapist's suggestions and encouragement to change thoughts and behaviour. This will affect the duration of therapy and require progress to be achieved in small increments with an emphasis on change being a positive experience.

The different cognitive and learning styles can include an enhanced ability to visualize such that therapy can be improved by using metaphor, especially if the metaphor is related to a client's interests. Research and clinical experience regarding the learning profile associated with autism confirms that many may have a prolonged cognitive processing time. Therapy must incorporate the extra time usually needed for an autistic client to intellectually process new information, perspectives and responses. This is often best achieved in silence. In agreement with the client, therapists may wish to include periods of silent intellectual processing within therapy sessions, and not to feel uncomfortable if no one is talking.

The autistic learning style may also include a fear of making mistakes and being judged and criticized by the therapist. This could inhibit or potentially terminate therapy, so it is important to have a positive approach to mistakes, sometimes called 'errorless learning'. A mistake is an opportunity to learn, not a sign of being stupid.

When socially engaged, an autistic client may have difficulties 'reading' people and social context and cues, (Theory of Mind), which affects the ability to make and keep friends. We have been describing for several decades the association between autism and impaired Theory of Mind, but a therapist may have difficulty 'reading' the autistic mind, and this reflects the Double Empathy problem. An autistic client may not clearly express their thoughts and feelings in speech (alexithymia) but also in non-verbal communication such as gestures, facial expressions, and tone of voice. There may be a genuine difficulty reading each other's thoughts.

Over time a therapist may be able to learn to 'read' their autistic client and vice versa, but there can be miscommunication and false assumptions. An autistic client may misinterpret the therapist's loud voice as an expression of anger rather than an adjustment of volume due to transitory background noise or the therapist may assume that a blank facial expression is a sign of a lack of comprehension.

The client's social history will probably include experiences of peer or work-colleague rejection, humiliation, bullying and teasing. This can lead to a generalized lack of trust, and it may take some time for an autistic client to trust the therapist and recognize their benevolent intentions.

Not knowing why someone behaved in a malicious way that caused distress, may lead an autistic client to obsessively ruminate on a specific event or the experience of social injustice, such that closure remains elusive. Therapy for an autistic client may include considerable time clarifying the motivations and intentions of others to achieve understanding, resolution, acceptance and forgiveness.

Autism is associated with chronic high anxiety levels, and one of the coping mechanisms for high anxiety is trying to control life experiences and maintain autonomy by avoiding demands experienced as overwhelming. An autistic client might perceive accepting therapy advice as surrendering autonomy to the therapist. Therapy can be adjusted to give the client choices to maintain a sense of autonomy and guide them to discover what they need to do rather than 'obey' the therapist.

The therapist must also determine if the autistic client's work and home life and suppressing and camouflaging autism are toxic to their mental health. Some environments are not 'autism friendly' with expectations that are difficult for the autistic person to achieve, a lack of understanding of autism in the family and workplace and expecting a level of socializing and endurance of aversive sensory experiences that contribute to autistic burnout. The therapist therefore has an ethical dilemma of using therapy and medication to encourage the tolerance of circumstances that will continue contributing to mental health issues, to put the client back in the 'lion's cage'. Therapy, as Steph Jones shows in this much needed book, can help determine the characteristics of an autism-friendly lifestyle and develop an autistic client's capacity to thrive rather than just survive. There may be the valuable creation of a new lifestyle with guidance and support from the therapist that increases resilience and authenticity.

Professor Tony Attwood
Attwood and Garnett Events

Context Guide for Professionals

As discussed in the first chapter of this book, this section is intended to be a handy training resource for professionals to easily understand where I am clearly describing autism to my therapist in sessions but they fail to identify the signs. It's also worth noting that throughout the other parts of my story (non-sessions) I am giving you insight into my autistic frame of reference, so please be mindful that if you hear similar things crop up in your work you may be sitting with a neurodivergent client.

Naturally my one autistic experience does not speak for everyone, but I have done my best to map examples to the diagnostic criteria wherever possible – you may find it useful to have these on hand as you go through the text to see if you can match them up since they may not be immediately obvious. If you are in doubt you can always contact me through my Instagram account (Autistic_Therapist).

FROM CHAPTER 1

Presenting self-image:

> What I say and how **they** interpret me seems to be at odds, and I get the sense they have me labelled as a 'difficult patient'. Through therapy, the image I have of myself is that of a person who is too sensitive, too reactive, too resistant, too independent, too much of a thinker. Overall, I see myself as too much.

Social anxiety and suspicion of others:

> I feel irritated that I have to pass the prying eyes of the staff who work there. Accountants and solicitors, that sort of thing – people who stop talking when you walk past the photocopier and make silent judgements on your Monday morning attire.

An appreciation for rules, structures and systems:

> It is 10:59am. Veronica has never let me in before 11 o'clock on the dot, and I reflect on how this sends a powerful message in therapy – we are teaching clients that boundaries matter. Such rules are there to impose a proper structure and purpose and make sure that everyone knows where they stand. I am quite happy with the formality of this arrangement, even if I do feel a bit like a dog waiting to eat a biscuit off its nose.

Sensory discomfort:

> Before I sit down on the massive throne-like chair with its ridiculously tall and uncomfortable back...

Example of scripting behaviours:

> I open the proceedings with my usual cheerful, 'Y'alright?' Such is the correct protocol if you grew up in the north of England.

Hyper-sensitivity to rejection – rejection sensitivity dysphoria:

> ...I feel like I've just been kicked in the stomach by a hormonal donkey.

> Veronica begins to pick fluff off her sleeve and raises her eyebrows. 'I work with patients from Manchester all the time and they don't say that. I've never met anyone who says that.'

> I am stunned by Veronica's snappy response to my polite attempt at a hello and feel crestfallen.

Autistic shutdown/sensory break/overwhelm:

> Her prickly tone has completely sent me under (she doesn't seem to know what that means either) and I feel myself drowning in 'the bad place'. I force myself to engage in conversation, trying with Jedi-like mind power to remember the well-prepared reasons I'm here in the first place, but I just can't get back on firm footing now – her vibe has knocked me off my axis.

> Annoyingly I find myself zoning out, vacantly gazing into the distance fixated on a tiny brown sparrow in a tree. I expect she thinks this performance is me sulking, being passive-aggressive, childishly refusing to communicate like an adult, but the truth is I cannot wade through the trance-like treacle which has accumulated in my brain and fake normalcy.

> I have been told that what is happening is something called

'dissociation' – an automatic nervous system trauma-based response – yet to me it can happen anytime. When it happens it's more like I've gone on a kind of power save mode yet still being completely present in my mind and body. Sometimes it feels quite nice and I can lose myself staring at a blank wall for a full hour in a kind of guru-level meditative state. I've noticed my little cousin do it too, but he hasn't even gone through any trauma. He's only five.

Difficulties with objects within the environment being out of place (needing familiar and correct systems to offset anxiety):

adjust my throne so that it is perfectly straight and parallel to her chair. I do this every week and at this stage I am not clear whether the cleaner arranges it at such an exasperating and **blatantly incorrect** angle or if Veronica is testing me. If my chair is not in the correct position all I can think about for the session is that the furniture is **wrong**.

FROM CHAPTER 2

Sensory overload:

'It's like… the aisles of the supermarket get **inside** my head, do you know what I mean? All the lights and sounds, it flips me out, makes me dizzy. All those rows of identical products beaming into my skull under flickering lights. The chatter, the metal trolley noises and bloody till beeps – eeesh! It's like needles in my brain, it's actually very painful.'

Honest and truthful style of communication, no hidden agenda:

I feel totally puzzled by her observation as I have never been anything but truthful in our sessions. It wouldn't serve me to avoid anything at these extortionate prices. And besides that's just not my style (in fact since I was tiny the world has instructed me to be **less honest** about what I'm thinking and feeling – apparently most people dislike the truth and prefer a lukewarm bowl of beat-around-the-bush word-soup.)

Preparing for social interactions and needing tools to help me remember what I need to say (difficulties with social reciprocity, memory recall):

Each week I come prepared with another exciting chapter in the history of Steph Jones in the hope that when she has gathered all the material something new and shiny will leap out and help me make sense of my life.

Acknowledging difficulties with everyday demands and vagueness of presenting issue:

I can't even describe it fully at this stage, on paper I'm doing well (house, tick, car, tick, career, tick, relationship, tick), but everything just seems so frickin' hard.

Social anxiety/awkwardness/confusion/masking/scripting:

When I was a teenager my mum felt it was important for me to start 'challenging my shyness' by doing more and more things like ordering for myself in a restaurant, which felt like a truly terrifying experience. I remember saying to Mum, 'What if I can't remember what to ask for?' and she would look at me as if that was the most ridiculous thing she'd ever heard. Even now, ordering a cheeseburger at McDonald's feels like an impossible game of sudoku (thank heavens for self-service machines...). I'm always ready with my opening lines (which I silently repeat to myself as I stand in the queue), but there will always be some advanced quantum physics-esque follow-up questions I am ill-prepared for which no doubt makes me look a bit simple. It's like other people can just manage the back-and-forth of everyday conversation without giving it any thought, but for me it seems like I'm living in an improvised comedy sketch.)

'I've spoken to my therapy supervisor about our sessions and **she** thinks I'm a classic case of complex PTSD. I've started reading up on the symptoms and I'm inclined to agree with her, I definitely tick all the boxes.'

Veronica narrows her crinkly eyes at me, which feels like she has just poured a truck load of molten metal into my abdomen. I have said the wrong thing. Again. I am often unclear about non-verbal inference (why can't people just say what they mean?!)

Social preference for being alone and whilst not an autistic trait as a generalization, not missing people is rather common (anecdotally) and may be an indication of alexithymia:

'I'm not afraid of being left on my own – in fact I prefer it!'
'I don't miss people...'

Routines and sameness – restrictive and repetitive behaviours:

I don't have an inconsistent sense of identity – in fact I am boringly predictable in routine, behaviour, and appearance, having not changed my wardrobe or hair-do since 1997.'
...one month wanting the same sandwich every single day but then out of nowhere never wanting to see a sandwich again as long as I live.

Sensory distress resulting in emotional dysregulation:

> I **do** have occasional angry outbursts – never with other people but certainly with inanimate household objects, like noisy teaspoons which accidentally crash onto the floor.

Taking words literally/linguistically particular:

> Although words are incredibly important to me (some might even call me pedantic)...

Acknowledging high degree of intuition and other autistic qualities:

> I navigate through life using a kind of sixth sense animal instinct – intuition, patterns and energies are all I need to work out a person's intentions. I have an uncanny knack for cold reading others and don't get why people say things like 'Ted seems lovely, doesn't he?' when it's blatantly obvious that Mr. Bundy is a deranged serial killer.

FROM CHAPTER 3

Needing to prepare for social interactions:

> So that I don't feel lost in sessions (sometimes my mind can go a bit blank, especially if we're conversationally darting about all over the place) I like to take in my prep-notes for the week. She doesn't seem to like this though, and apparently it doesn't fit with free association. Only, if I don't have my notes I can very easily feel steamrollered into discussions that I don't really understand or find applicable to my situation. Veronica tells me I must 'stop controlling the therapy' which is another indicator of my desire to 'avoid intimacy'. I put my pen down and start

to feel like the world's most overwhelmed waitress, trying to re-member everybody's order and terrified of dropping the plates.

The realities of having a very small social battery with autism due to the immense concentration and effort required to 'pass for normal' (masking):

I describe how one of the things I find difficult to comprehend is why I seem to have such a small social battery. 'It's as though I can be having a lovely time with friends, or out for a meal, or a drink or whatever, and then suddenly there is this internal collapse where I am desperate to go home.'

Describing a special interest (whilst not mentioned to Veronica directly, there is a failed attempt to try and involve her in a conversation on a topic about music unrelated to the topic of therapy):

Clearly my encyclopaedic knowledge of pop music is lost on her as without even acknowledging what I'd said...

Expressing alexithymia:

'What are you feeling now?' she asks, as if I'm some lab rat in an experiment.

'Nothing, really,' I respond with total sincerity.

'No, you can't feel nothing. That's simply not possible. You must feel something in this moment. Do you mean that you feel stunned? Empty? Annoyed?'

'No, not at all.' I reply. 'I feel full inside – whole, complete. Just stillness, really. Nothingness. The big space within that's eternally quiet. It isn't happy or sad, it's a place of no mind, of no feeling.'

Stimming (self-soothing behaviour) under stress:

> I close my eyes and start scratching my scalp with exploratory fingertips. I like doing this and feel there's nothing more satisfying than finding a bit in your hair and then flicking it away from under your fingernails.

FROM CHAPTER 5

Difficulties with everyday demands and tasks (executive dysfunction):

'I only had one thing to do this week, which by anyone else's standards doesn't seem to be that difficult at all.'

'What was it you had to do?' asked Veronica, with a furrowed brow you could keep pound coins in.

'I had to take a package back to the shop, for a return thing, you know, to Amazon, with the scanning machines, you know, the... things? I don't know what they're bloody called, scanning labelling posting machines?'

'Go on.'

'Well, things like that don't seem hard for other people but for me it felt like a total ordeal. First I had to **find** the package and make sure the bits were all inside, then I had to **leave the house** making sure I had all my bits and bobs with me like my keys, phone, purse... **then** I have to remind myself of what I'm going to say once I'm in the shop...'

Further evidence of scripting for social interactions:

'You have to **remind** yourself of what you are going to say? Why ever would you do that?'

I don't even understand the question. Doesn't everyone do that?

'Because if I don't, I'll forget and just stand there all blank and looking stupid.'

Sensory overwhelm/unfamiliar environment and processes needing a lot of cognitive 'in-real-time' processing, causing severe anxiety (on the verge of an autistic meltdown) and not feeling I have the capacity to handle the unexpected interaction:

Then there was so much traffic, and noise, and people passing by – I felt like I was going to have a panic attack. And then once I got in the shop I couldn't find the thingamabob machine. Then my QR code wasn't working and I was getting really upset and nearly started crying. Then the woman came to help me and was asking all these questions and I hadn't prepared any of those answers...

Black and white thinking/catastrophizing due to not being understood (frustration being a major meltdown trigger which lasted for several days – unable to self-regulate after negative interaction or recognize neurotypical friends' intentions/small talk/figures of speech):

'Well, actually they turned it into a joke, as if I was being funny. She said, "Nothing is ever easy!" And to be honest it induced what I can only describe as a venomous psychotic rage which lasted for days.'

'She made a joke and you got angry?' (Oh my God, woman, stop stating the obvious! I just bloody said that!!).

241

'Yes, I went crazy, just screaming and jumping up and down, my heart felt like it was going to explode. And when I'm like that I can't bring myself down again. It's like my temper is too big for my body. One time I actually thought I was having a stroke, but it's weird because I'm not an angry person at all. More of a peace loving hippy really.'

'But **why** did you feel so angry?'

'Because I feel like that's all I've had my entire life from others. I'm explaining how difficult I find the simplest of tasks, how going into a shop and returning a package feels like I'm stood in the middle of a Japanese train station without a map, and everyone just laughs it off. It's not funny and the invalidation, flippancy and minimization makes me want to hurt myself. I can't cope and I don't fucking know why.'

Childhood evidence of self-injurious behaviour and an inability to self-soothe:

I remember her trying to get me to do my maths homework and I stabbed myself with a pencil in frustration. One time I actually tried to hang myself with a dressing gown cord because I couldn't complete Super Mario Bros. Why are my emotions so much bigger than other people's...

Describing flat facial expressions:

...and yet my face doesn't really give any clear indication of how I'm feeling inside? It's like my brain and expressions aren't fully wired together and I've been told I have a good poker face on more than one occasion (maybe a potential career move).

Evidence of general clumsiness (difficulty with proprioception):

> As I reach over to the bottle of wine in the middle of the table I manage to knock Collette's glass all over her. How can one human being be so clumsy?! I'm convinced I haven't caught up with the new dimensions of being a fully-grown adult human and still think I'm five years old.

A need for perfection, order and correctness:

> I pour her a top-up doing silent counting in my head to make sure our glasses are both evenly distributed (anything else other than precision will bother me).

Social confusion and not understanding what is expected in sessions:

> Pregnant pauses filling the air with an acrid smoke she wanted me to do something with. Did she want me to say I'd miss her or something?

Rule-based self-governance which cannot be broken (running on logic rather than emotions and not giving self-permission to act on feelings):

> 'It's such a weird feeling but I feel almost naughty as if I'm not **allowed** to terminate sessions, much in the same way I've ended up staying in toxic relationships. I think I have a rule that it's rude to walk away from someone and that you should be nice if you are to not hurt their feelings.'

FROM CHAPTER 6

Conflict creating an autistic shutdown and rush of overwhelming emotions:

The trauma of the situation has made my body feel like lead, my head filled with a kind of white static that temporarily disables my thoughts.

Difficulties identifying feelings from an emotional perspective but noticing changes in body to give clues:

Back at my car, I get in, slump back in my chair and pull down the visor mirror. I feel okay but my eyes tell a different story, their usual light blue turning a shade of gunmetal. I do not feel any compulsion to scream or shout or cry, but there is a new sensation within me which I can only describe as a white hot seriousness. In that moment I am unable to correctly identify just how traumatic that situation was or recognize what long-lasting effect it will have on me. Always operating at a pragmatic, logical level, I figure it's done, over. Nothing left to see here, people, I'm driving home now.

How absolutely wrong I was.

About the Author

Steph Jones is an accredited psychotherapist, diagnostician, author and speaker specializing in autistic adults, highly sensitive people, dysfunctional families, complex trauma and emotional abuse. She is also proud to be autistic.

Her work has appeared in publications such as 'The Guardian', 'Metro', 'Therapy Today' (BACP), 'Psychotherapy and Politics International' (Wiley), 'Counselling Directory', 'The Counsellor's Café' magazine and 'Psychreg'. She runs the popular Instagram account Autistic_Therapist. Steph continues to provide psychological services to clients all around the world from her private practice in Manchester, UK, generally wearing fluffy slippers and a 20-year-old ripped Nirvana T-shirt.

References

American Psychiatric Association (2013) Diagnostic and Statistical Manual of Mental Disorders (5th edn) (DSM-5). Washington, DC: American Psychiatric Association.

Armstrong, T. (2015) 'The myth of the normal brain.' AMA Journal of Ethics 17, 4, 348–352. doi:10.1001/journalofethics.2015.17.4.msoc1-1504

Babb, C., Brede, J., Jones, C.R.G., Elliott, M. et al. (2021) '"It's not that they don't want to access the support... it's the impact of the autism": The experience of eating disorder services from the perspective of autistic women, parents and healthcare professionals.' Autism 25, 5, 1409–1421. doi:10.1177/1362361321991257

Baron-Cohen, S. (2002) 'The extreme male brain theory of autism.' Trends in Cognitive Sciences 6, 6, 248–254. doi:10.1016/s1364-6613(02)01904-6

Baron-Cohen, S. and Wheelwright, S. (2004) The empathy quotient: An investigation of adults with Asperger syndrome or high functioning autism, and normal sex differences. Journal of Autism and Developmental Disorders 34, 163–175. doi:10.1023/B:JADD.0000022607.19833.00

Baron-Cohen, S., Johnson, D., Asher, J., Wheelwright, S. et al. (2013) 'Is synaesthesia more common in autism?' Molecular Autism 4, 40. doi:10.1186/2040-2392-4-40

Black, M.H., Chen, N.T.M., Iyer, K.K., Lipp, O.V. et al. (2017) 'Mechanisms of facial emotion recognition in autism spectrum disorders: Insights from eye tracking and electroencephalography.' Neuroscience and Biobehavioral Reviews 80, 488–515. doi:10.1016/j.neubiorev.2017.06.016

Bleuler, E. (1950) Dementia Praecox or the Group of Schizophrenias. International Universities Press.

Booth, R. and Happé, F. (2010) '"Hunting with a knife and... fork": Examining central coherence in autism, attention deficit/hyperactivity disorder, and typical development with a linguistic task.' Journal of Experimental Child Psychology 107, 4, 377–393. doi: 10.1016/j.jecp.2010.06.003

Brach, T. (2003) Radical Acceptance. London: Rider.

Butwicka, A., Långström, N., Larsson, H., Lundström, S. et al. (2017) 'Increased risk for substance use-related problems in autism spectrum disorders: A population-based cohort study. Journal of Autism and Developmental Disorders 47, 80–89. doi:10.1007/s10803-016-2914-2

Camm-Crosbie, L., Bradley, L., Shaw, R., Baron-Cohen, S. and Cassidy, S. (2019) '"People like me don't get support": Autistic adults' experiences of support and treatment for mental health difficulties, self-injury and suicidality.' Autism 23, 6, 1431–1441. doi:10.1177/1362361318816053

Cassidy, S., Au-Yeung, S., Robertson, A., Cogger-Ward, H., et al. (2022) 'Autism and autistic traits in those who died by suicide in England.' British Journal of Psychiatry 221, 5, 683–691. doi:10.1192/bjp.2022.21

Cazalis, F., Reyes, E., Leduc, S. and Gourion, D. (2022) 'Evidence that nine autistic women out of ten have been victims of sexual violence.' Frontiers in Behavioral Neuroscience 16, 852203. doi:10.3389/fnbeh.2022.852203

Craft, S. (2012, 31 March) Females with Asperger's syndrome (non-official) checklist [Blog post]. Accessed on 3/8/2023 at https://everydayaspergers.com/2012/03/31/day-62-females-with-aspergers-syndrome-nonofficial-checklist

Crawford, M.J., Thana, L., Farquharson, L., Palmer, L. et al. (2016) 'Patient experience of negative effects of psychological treatment: Results of a national survey. British Journal of Psychiatry 208: 260–265. doi:10.1192/bjp.bp.114.162628

Cunningham Abbott, A. (2019) Counselling Adults with Autism. New York, NY: Routledge.

Desarkar, P., Rajji, T.K., Ameis, S.H. and Daskalakis, Z.J. (2015) 'Assessing and stabilizing aberrant neuroplasticity in autism spectrum disorder: The potential role of transcranial magnetic stimulation.' Frontiers of Psychiatry 6, 124. doi:10.3389/fpsyt.2015.00124

Elkins, D.N. (2016) The Human Elements of Psychotherapy: A Nonmedical Model of Emotional Healing. American Psychological Association Press.

Emanuel, C. (2015) 'An accidental Pokemon expert: Contemporary psychoanalysis on the autism spectrum.' International Journal of Psychoanalytic Self Psychology 10, 1, 53–68. doi:10.1080/15551024.2015.977485

Engineer, C.T., Hays, S.A. and Kilgard, M.P. (2017) 'Vagus nerve stimulation as a potential adjuvant to behavioral therapy for autism and other neurodevelopmental disorders.' Journal of Neurodevelopmental Disorders 9, 20. doi:10.1186/s11689-017-9203-z

Gennatas, E.D., Avants, B.B., Wolf, D.H., Satterthwaite, T.D. et al. (2017) 'Age-related effects and sex differences in gray matter density, volume, mass, and cortical thickness from childhood to young adulthood.' Journal of Neuroscience 37, 20, 5065–5073. doi:10.1523/JNEUROSCI.3550-16.2017

Haigh, S.M., Walsh, J.A., Mazefsky, C.A., Minshew, N.J. and Eack, S.M. (2018) 'Processing speed is impaired in adults with autism spectrum disorder, and relates to social communication abilities.' Journal of Autism and Developmental Disorders 48, 8, 2653–2662. doi:10.1007/s10803-018-3515-z

Hollocks, M., Lerh, J., Magiati, I., Meiser-Stedman, R. and Brugha, T. (2019) 'Anxiety and depression in adults with autism spectrum disorder: A systematic review and meta-analysis.' Psychological Medicine 49, 4, 559–572. doi:10.1017/S0033291718002283

Hudson, C.C., Hall, L. and Harkness, K.L.(2019) 'Prevalence of depressive disorders in individuals with autism spectrum disorder: A meta-analysis.' Journal of Abnormal Child Psychology 47, 165–175. doi:10.1007/s10802-018-0402-1

Jones, R.S.P., Quigney, C. and Huws, J.C. (2003) 'First-hand accounts of sensory perceptual experiences in autism: A qualitative analysis.' Journal of Intellectual and Developmental Disability 28, 2, 112–121.

Jones, S. (2018) 'Experts by experience.' Therapy Today 29, 2, 20–23.

Khalfa, S., Bruneau, N., Rogé, B., Georgieff, N. et al. (2004) 'Increased perception of loudness in autism.' Hearing Research 198, 1–2, 87–92.

Kinnaird, E., Stewart, C. and Tchanturia, K. (2019) 'Investigating alexithymia in autism: A systematic review and meta-analysis.' European Psychiatry 55, 80–89. doi:10.1016/j.eurpsy.2018.09.004

Kübler-Ross, E. (1969) On Death and Dying. Routledge.

Kumar, S., Reynolds, K., Ji, Y., Gu, R. et al. (2019) 'Impaired neurodevelopmental pathways in autism spectrum disorder: a review of signaling mechanisms and crosstalk.' Journal of Neurodevelopmental Disorders 11. doi:10.1186/s11689-019-9268-y

Kuppens, P., Tuerlinckx, F., Russell, J.A. and Barrett, L.F. (2013) 'The relation between valence and arousal in subjective experience.' Psychological Bulletin 139, 4, 917–940. doi:10.1037/a0030811

Lai, C.L.E., Lau, Z., Lui, S.S., Lok, E. et al. (2017) 'Meta-analysis of neuropsychological measures of executive functioning in children and adolescents with high-functioning autism spectrum disorder.' Autism Research 10, 5, 911–939. doi:10.1002/aur.1723

Langelaan, S/, Bakker, A.B., Schaufeli, W.B., van Rhenen, W. and van Doornen, L.J. (2007) 'Is burnout related to allostatic load?' International Journal of Behavioral Medicine 14, 4, 213–221. doi:10.1007/BF03002995

Lobregt-van Buuren, E., Hoekert, M. and Sizoo B. (2021) 'Autism, Adverse Events, and Trauma.' In A.M. Grabrucker (ed.) Autism Spectrum Disorders. Brisbane: Exon Publications. Available at www.ncbi.nlm.nih.gov/books/NBK573608

MacLennan, K., O'Brien, S. and Tavassoli, T. (2021) 'In our own words: The complex sensory experiences of autistic adults.' Journal of Autism and Developmental Disorders 52, 7, 3061–3075. doi:10.1007/s10803-021-05186-3

Maïano, C., Normand, C.L., Salvas, M-C., Moullec, G. and Aimé, A. (2015) 'Prevalence of school bullying among youth with autism spectrum disorders: A systematic review and meta-analysis.' Autism Research 9. doi:10.1002/aur.1568

Malone, K.M., Pearson, J.N., Palazzo, K.N., Manns, L.D. et al. (2022) 'The scholarly neglect of black autistic adults in autism Research.' Autism in Adulthood 4, 4, 271–280.

Martin, D.J., Garske, J.P. and Davis, M.K. (2000). 'Relation of the therapeutic alliance with outcome and other variables: A meta-analytic review.' Journal of Consulting and Clinical Psychology 68, 3, 438–450. doi:10.1037/0022-006X.68.3.43

McVey, A.J. (2019) 'The neurobiological presentation of anxiety in autism spectrum disorder: A systematic review.' Autism Research 12, 3, 346–369. doi:10.1002/aur.2063

Milton, D.E.M. (2012) 'On the ontological status of autism: The "double empathy problem".' Disability & Society 27, 6, 883–887. doi:10.1080/09687599.2012.710008

Minshew, N.J. and Williams, D.L. (2007) 'The new neurobiology of autism: Cortex, connectivity, and neuronal organization.' Archives of Neurology 64, 7, 945–950.

Nagoski, E. and Nagoski, A. (2019) Burnout: Solve Your Stress Cycle. London: Vermilion.

National Autistic Society (2022) Number of autistic people in mental health hospitals: Latest data. Accessed on 21/6/2023 at www.autism.org.uk/what-we-do/news/autistic-people-in-mental-health-hospitals

National Institute for Health and Care Excellence (2021) Autism Spectrum Disorder in Adults: Diagnosis and Management. Clinical Guidance (CG142). Accessed on 2/8/2023 qt www.nice.org.uk/guidance/cg142

NHS England (2022) LDA monthly statistics from the Assuring Transformation dataset. Accessed on 21/6/2023 at https://digital.nhs.uk/data-and-information/publications/statistical/learning-disability-services-statistics/at-january-2022-mhsds-november-2021-final/datasets---at

Norcross, J. (2002) Psychotherapy Relationships That Work. New York: Oxford University Press.

Obaydi, H. and Puri, B.K. (2008) 'Prevalence of premenstrual syndrome in autism: A prospective observer-rated study.' Journal of International Medical Research 36, 2, 268–272. doi: 10.1177/147323000803600208

Pavăl, D. (2017) 'A dopamine hypothesis of autism spectrum disorder.' Developmental Neuroscience 39, 355–360. doi:10.1159/000478725

Pearson, A., Rose, K. and Rees, J. (2022, May 12). '"Professionals are the hardest to trust" Supporting autistic adults who have experienced interpersonal victimisation.' [Preprint]. doi.org/10.31219/osf.io/5y8jw

Pidd, H. (2022) 'Autistic girl, 14, unlawfully detained in hospital, high court judge finds.' The Guardian, 5 April 2022 Accessed on 21/6/2023 at www.theguardian.com/uk-news/2022/apr/05/autistic-girl-14-unlawfully-detained-hospital-high-court-judge-finds

Raymaker, D.M., Teo, A.R., Steckler, N.A., Lentz, B. et al. (2020) '"Having all of your internal resources exhausted beyond measure and being left with no clean-up crew": Defining autistic burnout.' Autism in Adulthood 2, 2, 132–143. doi.org/10.1089/aut.2019.

Remington, A.M., Swettenham, J.G. and Lavie, N. (2012) 'Lightening the load: Perceptual load impairs visual detection in typical adults but not in autism.' Journal of Abnormal Psychology 121, 2, 544–551. doi:10.1037/a0027670

Rogers, C. (1957) 'The necessary and sufficient conditions of therapeutic personality change.' Journal of Consulting Psychology 21, 95–103.

Rutigliano, G., Rocchetti, M., Paloyelis, Y., Gilleen, J. et al. (2016) 'Peripheral oxytocin and vasopressin: Biomarkers of psychiatric disorders? A comprehensive systematic review and preliminary meta-analysis.' Psychiatry Research 241, 207–220. doi:10.1016/j.psychres.2016.04.117

Rutter, M. (1972) 'Childhood schizophrenia reconsidered.' Journal of Autism & Childhood Schizophrenia 2, 4, 315–337.

Safran, J.D., Muran, J.C., Wallner Samstag, L. and Stevens, C. (2001) 'Repairing alliance ruptures.' Psychotherapy: Theory, Research, Practice, Training 38, 406–412. doi:10.1037/0033-3204.38.4.406

Sedgewick, F., Hull, L. and Ellis, H. (2022) Autism and Masking: How and Why People Do It, and the Impact It Can Have. London: Jessica Kingsley Publishers.

Sheppard, E., Pillai, D., Wong, G.T-L., Ropar, D. and Mitchell, P. (2016) 'How easy is it to read the minds of people with autism spectrum disorder?' Journal of Autism and Developmental Disorders 46, 1247–1254 (2016). doi:10.1007/s10803-015-2662-8

Siegel, D. (2015) The Developing Mind: How Relationships and the Brain Interact to Shape Who We Are. New York, NY: Guilford Press.

Simonoff, E., Pickles, A., Charman, T., Chandler, S. et al. (2008) 'Psychiatric disorders in children with autism spectrum disorders: Prevalence, comorbidity, and associated factors in a population-derived sample.' Journal of the American Academy of Child and Adolescent Psychiatry 47, 8, 921–929. doi:10.1097/CHI.0b013e318179964f

South, M., Costa, A.P. and McMorris, C. (2021) 'Death by suicide among people with autism: Beyond zebrafish.' JAMA Network Open 4, 1, e2034018. doi:10.1001/jamanetworkopen.2020.34018

Stagg, S.D. and Belcher, H. (2019) 'Living with autism without knowing: Receiving a diagnosis in later life.' Health Psychology and Behavioral Medicine 7, 1, 348–361. doi:10.1080/21642850.2019.1684920

Taylor, S.E. (1983) 'Adjustment to threatening events: A theory of cognitive adaptation.' American Psychologist 38, 11, 1161–1173. doi:10.1037/0003-066X.38.11.1161

Tennov, D. (1979) Love and Limerence. Lanham, MD: Scarborough House.

Thapa, R., Alvares, G.A., Zaidi, T.A., Thomas, E.E. et al. (2019) 'Reduced heart rate variability in adults with autism spectrum disorder.' Autism Research 12, 6, 922–930. doi:10.1002/aur.2104

Valnegri, P., Huang, J., Yamada, T., Yang, Y. et al. (2017) 'RNF8/UBC13 ubiquitin signaling suppresses synapse formation in the mammalian brain.' Nature Communications, 2 November 2017.

van der Kolk, B.A. (2014) The Body Keeps the Score: Brain, Mind, and Body in the Healing of Trauma. Viking.

Vecchiato, M., Sacchi, C., Simonelli, A. and Purgato, N. (2016) 'Evaluating the efficacy of psychodynamic treatment on a single case of autism. A qualitative research.' Research in Psychotherapy: Psychopathology, Process and Outcome. doi:10.4081/ripppo.2016.194

Walker, P. (2013) Complex PTSD: From Surviving to Thriving. Azure Coyote.

Subject Index

Author Index